THE GREEN WITCH'S HERBAL

A Practical Guide to Magical Herbs, Natural Remedies, and Green Witchcraft

VIVIENNE GRANT

Copyright © 2025 by Vivienne Grant

The content contained within this book may not be reproduced, duplicated or transmitted without direct written permission from the author or the publisher.

Under no circumstances will any blame or legal responsibility be held against the publisher, or author, for any damages, reparation, or monetary loss due to the information contained within this book. Either directly or indirectly. You are responsible for your own choices, actions, and results.

Legal Notice:

This book is copyright protected. This book is only for personal use. You cannot amend, distribute, sell, use, quote or paraphrase any part, or the content within this book, without the consent of the author or publisher.

Disclaimer Notice:

Please note the information contained within this document is for educational and entertainment purposes only. All effort has been executed to present accurate, up to date, and reliable, complete information. No warranties of any kind are declared or implied. Readers acknowledge that the author is not engaging in the rendering of legal, financial, medical or professional advice. The content within this book has been derived from various sources. Please consult a licensed professional before attempting any techniques outlined in this book.

By reading this document, the reader agrees that under no circumstances is the author responsible for any losses, direct or indirect, which are incurred as a result of the use of the information contained within this document, including, but not limited to, — errors, omissions, or inaccuracies.

CONTENTS

Introduction: The Living Magic of Plants ... vii

1. THE HISTORICAL ROOTS OF HERBAL MAGIC ... 1
   The Ancient Origins of Magical Herbalism ... 1
   From Folk Magic to Modern Practice ... 4
   Notable Herbalists Through History ... 7

2. UNDERSTANDING PLANT ENERGETICS ... 11
   The Doctrine of Signatures ... 11
   Elemental Associations of Plants ... 14
   Planetary and Astrological Correspondences ... 17

3. CULTIVATING MAGICAL RELATIONSHIPS WITH PLANTS ... 22
   Creating a Witch's Garden ... 22
   Communication and Connection with Plant Spirits ... 26
   Ethical Wildcrafting Practices ... 29

4. THE MAGICAL APOTHECARY: ESSENTIAL HERBS ... 35
   Protective Herbs for Magical Safety ... 36
   Herbs for Healing and Wellness Magic ... 40
   Manifestation and Prosperity Plants ... 44

5. ADVANCED HERBAL CORRESPONDENCES ... 50
   Magical Properties of Trees and Woods ... 50
   Magical Uses of Roots and Underground Plants ... 55
   Flowers, Seeds, and Fruits in Magic ... 59

6. CREATING MAGICAL HERBAL PREPARATIONS ... 65
   Drying and Storing Magical Herbs ... 65
   Herbal Oils, Tinctures, and Extracts ... 70
   Powders, Incense, and Smoking Blends ... 74

7. HERBAL TOOLS AND TALISMANS ... 80
   Crafting Herbal Charm Bags and Sachets ... 81
   Crafting Herbal Wands, Staffs, and Ritual Tools ... 86
   Living Plant Talismans and Guardians ... 92

8. KITCHEN WITCHCRAFT WITH HERBS ... 99
   Magical Cooking and Baking with Herbs ... 100
   Brewing Magical Teas and Potions ... 105
   Herbal Honeys, Vinegars, and Preserves ... 111

9. HERBAL MAGIC THROUGHOUT THE SEASONS ... 117
   Spring Herbs and Renewal Rituals ... 118
   Summer Abundance and Solar Herbs ... 123
   Autumn Harvests and Transformative Plant Magic ... 130

10. HERBAL RITUALS AND CEREMONIES ... 138
    Herbal Cleansing and Purification Rituals ... 139
    Herbs for Life Transitions and Rites of Passage ... 145
    Seasonal Herbal Altar Practices ... 152

11. HEALING APPLICATIONS OF MAGICAL HERBALISM ... 159
    Creating a Magical Herbal First Aid Kit ... 160
    Herbs for Emotional and Psychological Support ... 167
    Spiritual Cleansing and Protective Herbal Baths ... 172

12. ADVANCED HERBAL MAGIC TECHNIQUES ... 180
    Working with Plant Spirits and Deities ... 181
    Dream Work and Divination with Herbs ... 187
    Shamanic Plant Practices ... 194

Growing Your Herbal Craft

INTRODUCTION: THE LIVING MAGIC OF PLANTS

In the quiet of a forest at dawn, in the sunny corner of an urban garden, or in the small pot on a city windowsill—wherever plants grow, a magical connection awaits awakening. This connection represents one of humanity's oldest magical bonds, a green thread woven through the very fabric of witchcraft history and spiritual practices.

THE ANCIENT RELATIONSHIP BETWEEN WITCHES AND PLANTS

Since time immemorial, witches have intertwined their fate with the plant kingdom. This relationship was never merely pragmatic, but deeply spiritual and reciprocal. The witch and the herb have danced together through centuries—the witch offering care, reverence, and intention; the plant offering healing, protection, and transformation in return.

Ancient cave paintings depict plant-wielding shamanic figures. Archaeological discoveries reveal plant remains in ritual contexts dating back thousands of years. From the cunning folk of medieval Europe to the curanderos of Latin America, from the shamans of indigenous tribes to the village wise women, those who walked between worlds did so with plants as their steadfast allies.

This ancient bond was forged through careful observation, intuitive connection, and generations of accumulated wisdom. The witch's knowledge of plants transcended the merely medicinal—it encompassed an understanding of plants as sentient beings with whom one could communicate, negotiate, and form alliances. This perspective, once dismissed as superstition, finds increasing validation in modern biological research revealing the complex communication networks and intelligence of plant life.

HOW PLANTS FORM THE BACKBONE OF HISTORICAL MAGICAL PRACTICE

Throughout history, magical practitioners relied on plants as the primary tools of their craft. The herbalist's garden and the witch's cupboard contained the essential ingredients for virtually every magical operation. From protection to prosperity, from healing to hexing, from divination to devotion—plants provided the material basis for magical work across cultures and traditions.

Historical grimoires and magical texts reveal the centrality of herbs in magical practice. The Greek Magical Papyri, medieval Books of Shadows, and Renaissance texts like Culpeper's Herbal all catalog extensive botanical knowledge intertwined with magical instruction. Plants were burned as incense to carry prayers to deities, crafted into amulets for protection, steeped in ritual baths for purification, and incorporated into foods and drinks for healing and transformation.

The witch's garden was both pharmacy and temple—a sacred space where magical ingredients were cultivated with intention and harvested with reverence. The rhythms of planting, tending, and harvesting connected practitioners to the cycles of nature, grounding magical work in the tangible reality of earth's abundance.

THE MODERN REVIVAL OF HERBAL WITCHCRAFT

In recent decades, we've witnessed a remarkable resurgence of interest in herbal magic. This revival emerges from multiple streams: a growing disillusionment with industrial approaches to medicine and agriculture, an increasing ecological awareness, and a hunger for spiritual practices that connect us directly to the natural world.

Modern green witches draw inspiration from historical practices while adapting them to contemporary contexts. Urban apartment dwellers cultivate magical windowsill gardens. Suburban witches transform conventional lawns into productive magical landscapes. Rural practitioners revive traditional wildcrafting with a renewed emphasis on sustainability and reciprocity.

This revival has been facilitated by improved access to

botanical knowledge through books, workshops, and online communities. The modern witch has unprecedented opportunities to learn about plants from diverse traditions around the world while developing a localized practice rooted in their specific bioregion.

Today's herbal witch practices at the intersection of ancient wisdom and modern understanding—informed by traditional lore but enhanced by scientific knowledge about plant properties, sustainable harvesting methods, and ecological relationships. This synthesis creates a magical practice that is both deeply rooted and thoroughly contemporary.

HOW THIS BOOK WILL GUIDE YOUR HERBAL PRACTICE DEVELOPMENT

This comprehensive guide aims to walk beside you on your journey into herbal magic, whether you're taking your first steps or seeking to deepen an established practice. Throughout these pages, we'll explore both theoretical foundations and practical applications, historical context and contemporary innovations.

We begin by examining the historical roots of herbal magic, providing context for understanding the rich traditions from which modern practice emerges. From there, we explore the energetic qualities of plants—how to work with their elemental, planetary, and intrinsic magical signatures.

The heart of this book focuses on practical skills: cultivating magical relationships with plants, creating an extensive magical apothecary, crafting effective herbal preparations, and incorporating plants into rituals throughout the seasons. Special attention is given to ethical considerations, including sustainable harvesting, appropriate cultural exchange, and environmental stewardship.

Advanced chapters delve into specialized applications: working with plant spirits, herbs for healing on multiple levels, dream work, divination, and ceremonial applications. Throughout, you'll find specific recipes, rituals, and techniques you can immediately incorporate into your practice, along with prompts for developing your unique approach to herbal magic.

By the conclusion of this journey together, you'll possess not only a wealth of practical knowledge but also the foundation for a deeply personal, ethical, and effective magical relationship with the plant kingdom.

SETTING REALISTIC EXPECTATIONS FOR HERBAL MAGIC

As we embark on this exploration of herbal magic, it's important to approach the work with clear understanding of both its potential and its limitations. Plant magic is powerful, but it operates according to its own nature and timeline.

Herbal magic tends to unfold gradually, like the growth of a plant itself—a seedling doesn't become a mature tree overnight, nor do most herbal workings manifest instantaneously. The magic of plants excels in areas aligned with natural processes: healing, growth, transformation, protection, purification, and connection. It rarely produces the dramatic, immediate effects portrayed in popular media.

Effective herbal magic requires patience, consistency, and relationship. Results come from regular practice, careful observation, and genuine connection with plant allies. This is not a practice of domination—commanding plants to fulfill our wishes—but of collaboration, working in harmony with the inherent qualities and energies of our botanical partners.

Additionally, herbal magic works best when supported by practical action. A healing ritual supports but doesn't replace appropriate medical care. A prosperity working enhances but doesn't substitute for sound financial decisions. The most effective magical practitioners understand this complementary relationship between magical work and practical steps.

Finally, developing skill with herbal magic requires both study and direct experience. The knowledge contained in these pages provides essential foundations, but your personal relationships with plants—cultivated through growing, harvesting, preparing, and working with them directly—will be your most profound teacher.

With realistic expectations and a commitment to developing authentic relationships with plants, you'll discover that herbal magic offers a deeply rewarding path—one that connects you to ancient traditions while responding to the unique challenges and opportunities of our contemporary world. As we proceed, may you find not only practical skills but a deepened sense of connection to the green beings who share our planet and have so much wisdom to offer.

CHAPTER 1

THE HISTORICAL ROOTS OF HERBAL MAGIC

To understand modern herbal magic is to trace a green thread through human history, following the intricate ways our ancestors interacted with the plant kingdom. This botanical relationship extends far beyond simple utilization—it reveals a complex tapestry of reverence, empirical discovery, and magical belief that has shaped how we relate to plants today. By examining this rich historical context, we gain not only appreciation for those who preserved this knowledge through difficult times but also deeper insight into the foundations of contemporary practice.

THE ANCIENT ORIGINS OF MAGICAL HERBALISM

The relationship between humans and plants as magical allies predates written history. Archaeological evidence from Paleolithic sites reveals careful placement of medicinal plants in burial contexts, suggesting early recognition of plants' spiritual as well as physical properties. In the Shanidar Cave in Iraq, a Neanderthal burial from approximately 60,000 BCE contained pollen from eight medicinal plants, several of which continue to appear in modern herbal formularies. This discovery suggests that even our evolutionary cousins may have recognized special properties in certain plants beyond their nutritional value.

As human societies developed, this intuitive relationship with plants became increasingly formalized. By the time of the earliest written records, sophisticated systems of herbal magic had already evolved across the globe. The Ebers Papyrus from Egypt (c. 1550 BCE) documents over 700 herbal formulas, many incorporating magical incantations alongside physical preparation instructions. This integration of the physical and metaphysical reflects the holistic worldview that characterized ancient herbal practice—a perspective in which healing the body could not be separated from addressing spiritual and energetic imbalances.

Similar evidence emerges across ancient civilizations. Sumerian clay tablets describe ritual uses for plants alongside medicinal applications. Chinese texts from the Han Dynasty detail the spiritual qualities of herbs that would later become incorporated into traditional Chinese medicine. The Rigveda of ancient India mentions the god Soma, whose identity appears connected to a sacred plant used in religious ceremony. The Greek physician Dioscorides cataloged over 600 medicinal plants in his De Materia Medica (c. 70 CE), including magical properties and ritual harvesting instructions for many.

Shamanic plant practices represent perhaps the most widespread ancient approach to magical herbalism. Across continents and climates, indigenous spiritual specialists developed intimate relationships with the plant kingdom, particularly with species that facilitated altered states of consciousness. These plants weren't viewed merely as tools but as teachers and spirits with whom the shaman could communicate directly. From the ayahuasca traditions of the Amazon to the use of sacred mushrooms in Mesoamerica, from the fly agaric rituals of Siberia to the red ochre and herbal mixtures of Southern African rock art sites, shamanic herbalism established core principles that continue to influence magical practitioners today: the importance of relationship with plant spirits, the role of intention in harvesting and preparation, and the understanding of plants as conscious allies rather than passive materials.

This ancient herbal knowledge wasn't preserved in books but transmitted through oral tradition. Elders taught apprentices through direct experience, seasonal observation, and memorized knowledge frameworks. These oral traditions incorporated songs, stories, and ceremonial practices that encoded practical information about plant identification, harvesting methods, preparation techniques, and magical applications. The intergenerational transmission of this knowledge required both teachers and students to develop exceptional observational skills and memory capacity, creating systems of botanical understanding that were simultaneously practical, spiritual, and ecological.

FROM FOLK MAGIC TO MODERN PRACTICE

As agricultural civilizations expanded, herbal knowledge developed along two parallel paths: the formal, often written traditions of scholars, physicians, and religious specialists; and the practical, largely oral traditions of village herbalists, midwives, and folk healers. These paths sometimes intersected but often developed distinct approaches to plant knowledge and use.

The Medieval period in Europe saw the preservation of much classical herbal knowledge through monastic traditions. Monastery gardens cultivated medicinal and magical herbs, while monks copied and translated ancient texts. Hildegard von Bingen (1098-1179), a German Benedictine abbess, wrote extensively about the medicinal and spiritual properties of plants, integrating classical knowledge with Christian symbolism and her own visionary experiences. Her writings exemplify the medieval European approach to plants, which often interpreted their properties through religious frameworks while maintaining practical applications derived from older traditions.

Outside monastery walls, folk herbalism thrived in rural communities through the work of village healers. These practitioners—predominantly women—maintained extensive knowledge of local plants and their applications for healing, protection, fertility, and other community needs. Their approach typically integrated practical observations with magical beliefs, embodying a worldview in which the material and spiritual realms were inextricably interconnected.

The Renaissance period brought renewed interest in ancient knowledge, including herbal lore. Herbals—illustrated books describing plants and their uses—became increasingly popular. Nicholas Culpeper's Complete Herbal (1653) represented a significant development, incorporating astrological correspondences with botanical descriptions and medicinal applications. This systematic linking of plants to planetary influences created a coherent magical framework that continues to influence modern herbal magic.

The grimoire tradition also flowered during this period, with magical texts often including extensive sections on plant magic. Works like the Key of Solomon contained detailed instructions for gathering herbs according to planetary hours, preparing them with appropriate incantations, and incorporating them into talismans and ritual objects. These texts codified magical herbalism into increasingly structured systems, though they often remained accessible only to the literate elite.

This flourishing of herbal knowledge faced a devastating setback with the witch persecutions that swept Europe and colonial America. The European witch hunts (roughly 1450-1750) specifically targeted those with herbal knowledge, particularly women who maintained folk healing traditions outside official religious and medical structures. Court records show that possession of herbal remedies frequently appeared as evidence of witchcraft, and many accused witches were local healers and midwives.

The human cost was enormous—tens of thousands executed—but equally significant was the loss of botanical knowledge. Practitioners went underground, stopped teaching apprentices, or abandoned their herbal work entirely. Many traditional plant uses were lost or fragmented as oral transmission chains were broken. Some knowledge survived in remote areas less affected by persecutions, while other traditions were preserved through written records or by practitioners who disguised magical applications as purely medicinal or culinary.

The scientific revolution and subsequent Enlightenment further marginalized magical approaches to plants. The mechanistic worldview that emerged separated the material properties of herbs from their spiritual aspects, privileging chemical analysis over traditional knowledge systems. By the 19th century, herbal magic had largely retreated to rural communities and private practice, while mainstream medicine increasingly turned toward isolated chemical compounds rather than whole plant preparations.

The revival of interest in magical herbalism began in the late 19th century, accelerating through the 20th century alongside various occult revivals, back-to-nature movements, and eventually the modern Pagan renaissance. Key figures in this revival included esoteric societies like the Hermetic Order of the Golden Dawn, which incorporated herbal correspondences into ceremonial magic; early feminist reclamations of witchcraft as empowering women's spirituality; and ecological movements that sought to restore respectful relationships with the natural world.

Today's practice represents a reconstruction and reimagining of historical traditions, informed by both ancient sources and contemporary insights. Modern herbal witches draw from surviving folk traditions, archaeological evidence, historical texts, and cross-cultural exchange, creating approaches that honor traditional wisdom while responding to current needs and understandings.

NOTABLE HERBALISTS THROUGH HISTORY

Throughout history, certain individuals have made exceptional contributions to the preservation and development of herbal knowledge. Their work forms the foundation upon which modern magical herbalism builds, providing both practical information and philosophical frameworks that continue to resonate.

Imhotep (c. 2650-2600 BCE), the Egyptian polymath, left some of the earliest written records of herbal medicine. Deified after his death, he became associated with healing magic and herbal wisdom in Egyptian tradition. The Edwin Smith Papyrus, possibly based on his teachings, contains sophisticated botanical remedies integrated with magical incantations.

In ancient Greece, Theophrastus (c. 371-287 BCE) produced the first systematic botanical works in Western tradition. His Historia Plantarum classified over 500 plant species and included information on their magical as well as medicinal properties. His student Aristotle further developed systematic approaches to understanding plants, influencing botanical knowledge for centuries.

The Roman naturalist Pliny the Elder (23-79 CE) compiled extensive information on plant uses in his Natural History, including magical applications alongside scientific observations. Pliny often expressed skepticism about supernatural claims while nonetheless documenting them thoroughly, creating an invaluable record of Roman-era plant magic.

During the Islamic Golden Age, Persian polymath Ibn Sina (Avicenna, 980-1037) produced The Canon of Medicine, synthesizing Greek, Arabic, and Persian knowledge of medicinal plants. Though primarily focused on medicinal rather than magical applications, his systematic approach to plant properties and planetary correspondences influenced later magical herbalism throughout Europe and the Middle East.

The 12th-century healer and visionary Hildegard von Bingen deserves special recognition for her works Physica and Causae et Curae, which detail hundreds of plants and their applications. Hildegard's approach integrated empirical observation with spiritual insight, describing the energetic qualities of plants alongside their physical effects. Her concept of "viriditas"—the divine life force manifesting as the green energy within plants—offers a profound philosophical foundation for understanding plant magic.

The Renaissance herbalist Nicholas Culpeper (1616-1654) revolutionized herbal practice by publishing his Complete Herbal in English rather than Latin, making plant knowledge accessible to common people. His systematic association of plants with planetary rulers and astrological influences created a coherent magical framework that continues to influence modern practice. Culpeper faced significant persecution from the medical establishment for democratizing herbal knowledge and challenging physician authority.

During the 19th century, the Eclectic physicians of America preserved and developed herbal knowledge when mainstream medicine increasingly abandoned botanical remedies. Practitioners like John King and Harvey Wickes Felter documented extensive information about American plants, integrating indigenous knowledge with European traditions. Though the Eclectics minimized the explicitly magical aspects of herbalism, their detailed observations of plant properties and energetics provide valuable information for modern magical practitioners.

Juliette de Bairacli Levy (1912-2009) traveled extensively throughout the Mediterranean, Middle East, and Europe, learning traditional herbal practices from local healers and shepherds. Her books brought these traditions to wider audiences and emphasized an ecological approach to herbalism that recognized the importance of wildcrafted herbs grown in their natural habitats. Her work bridges traditional knowledge and modern practice, preserving techniques that might otherwise have been lost.

Contemporary herbalist Rosemary Gladstar has been instrumental in the modern herbal renaissance, founding several herbal schools and organizations while authoring influential books that have introduced countless practitioners to herbal wisdom. Though not explicitly focused on magical applications, her emphasis on developing personal relationships with plants and understanding their energetic properties aligns closely with magical herbalism.

These historical figures preserved essential knowledge during periods when herbal wisdom was devalued or actively suppressed. Their written works provide valuable windows into past practices, while their life experiences demonstrate the challenges faced by those who maintained plant knowledge outside dominant paradigms. By studying their contributions, modern practitioners gain both practical information and deeper appreciation for the continuous thread of herbal wisdom through human history.

The historical roots of herbal magic remind us that our contemporary practice doesn't exist in isolation but forms part of humanity's ongoing relationship with the plant kingdom. This relationship has evolved through countless generations of observation, experimentation, intuition, and transmission. As modern practitioners, we inherit both the practical knowledge and the ethical responsibilities of this lineage—to use plants with respect, to honor the traditions that preserved this wisdom, and to continue developing approaches that respond to the unique challenges of our time.

CHAPTER 2

UNDERSTANDING PLANT ENERGETICS

To work effectively with plants in magical practice requires more than botanical identification or knowledge of physical properties. It demands an understanding of plant energetics—the subtle qualities, affinities, and resonances that determine how a plant functions in magical contexts. These energetic properties form the foundation for effective herbal magic, guiding practitioners in selecting and combining plants for specific magical purposes. This chapter explores three primary frameworks for understanding plant energetics: the Doctrine of Signatures, elemental associations, and planetary correspondences.

THE DOCTRINE OF SIGNATURES

The Doctrine of Signatures represents one of the oldest and most intuitive systems for understanding plant energetics.

This principle, formalized by Paracelsus in the 16th century but practiced in various forms across cultures for millennia, suggests that plants reveal their magical and medicinal properties through their physical characteristics. In essence, the plant's appearance, habitat, growth pattern, and other observable traits provide "signatures" indicating their magical affinities and applications.

This principle is elegantly summarized in the words of medieval herbalist William Coles: "The mercy of God... maketh... herbs for the use of men, and hath... given them particular signatures, whereby a man may read... the use of them." The doctrine does not suggest mere superficial resemblance but rather proposes that a plant's physical form reflects its essential nature and purpose within the greater order of creation.

The most straightforward signatures relate to physical resemblance. Plants with heart-shaped leaves, such as linden and violet, traditionally address heart-related concerns—not just physical heart ailments but emotional matters of the heart as well. Walnuts, with their brain-like appearance when removed from the shell, are associated with intelligence and mental clarity in magical work. Yellow flowers like calendula and dandelion, resembling the sun and its golden light, carry solar energy useful for confidence, vitality, and illumination spells.

Habitat provides another key signature. Plants that thrive in wet environments, such as willow growing alongside streams or lotus rising from muddy waters, connect energetically to emotional fluidity, intuition, and the subconscious.

Desert plants that survive in harsh conditions—sage, juniper, and various cacti—carry protective and purifying energies, helping to create boundaries and cleanse negative influences. Plants that grow in liminal spaces between environments, like blackberry brambles at forest edges, facilitate magical work involving transitions, thresholds, and communication between worlds.

Growth patterns reveal further magical correspondences. Vining plants that reach and climb, such as morning glory or ivy, excel in spells for aspiration, achievement, and overcoming obstacles. Plants with deep taproots, like dandelion and burdock, help to access deep truths, ancestral connections, and hidden knowledge. Fast-growing plants like bamboo or mint amplify energies of prosperity and abundance.

Sensory qualities constitute particularly potent signatures. Bitter herbs often serve protective functions in magic, keeping away unwanted energies just as their taste repels in the physical realm. Sweet-scented flowers like rose and jasmine attract love and pleasure. Sharp, aromatic herbs such as rosemary and thyme cut through confusion and illusion, bringing clarity and focus to magical workings.

The timing of a plant's growth cycle provides temporal signatures. Spring ephemerals that appear briefly before the forest canopy leafs out—bloodroot, trillium, and spring beauty—facilitate new beginnings, inspiration, and initiation. Plants that bloom at night, such as evening primrose or moonflower, naturally align with lunar magic, dreams, and the unconscious mind. Plants that retain their leaves through winter, like holly and pine, carry energies of perseverance, protection during difficult times, and the promise of renewal.

While the Doctrine of Signatures offers valuable insights, modern practitioners recognize both its usefulness and limitations. The system works best as one component of plant understanding rather than the sole determinant of magical properties. Contemporary herbalists interpret signatures contextually, considering ecological relationships, chemical constituents, and traditional uses alongside physical appearances. This balanced approach honors traditional wisdom while incorporating modern understanding of plant biology and chemistry.

The Doctrine of Signatures remains particularly valuable for developing personal relationships with plants. By carefully observing a plant's physical characteristics and habitat, practitioners attune to its unique energetic qualities. This observational practice trains magical sensitivity and intuition, helping witches recognize the subtle energetic differences between plants that might appear botanically similar but serve distinct magical functions.

ELEMENTAL ASSOCIATIONS OF PLANTS

The four classical elements—Earth, Air, Fire, and Water—provide another essential framework for understanding plant energetics. This elemental system originates in ancient Greek philosophy but appears in various forms across cultures worldwide. In magical herbalism, elemental associations help practitioners comprehend how plants interact with fundamental

UNDERSTANDING PLANT ENERGETICS

energetic forces and how they might be combined to create balanced or specifically targeted magical effects.

Earth plants ground energy, provide stability, and connect to material prosperity and physical healing. These plants typically have strong root systems, grow close to the ground, or produce substantial fruits, nuts, or tubers. Oak, with its deep roots and solid presence, exemplifies Earth energy at its most stable and enduring. Other Earth-associated plants include wheat, corn, and root vegetables that nourish the body; patchouli, whose heavy scent centers awareness in the physical; and ivy, which clings and stabilizes. Earth plants excel in magic for abundance, security, fertility, and establishing boundaries.

Air plants facilitate movement, communication, mental clarity, and intellectual pursuits. These often have delicate, windblown seeds; feathery leaves; or strong aromatic qualities that travel through the air. Dandelion, with its puffball seeds carried on the breeze, embodies the dispersive quality of Air. Lavender, whose scent uplifts and clarifies, stimulates Air's intellectual properties. Wind-pollinated trees like pine create connections across distances. Air plants strengthen spells for learning, divination, travel, freedom, and enhancing mental abilities.

Fire plants stimulate energy, passion, courage, transformation, and purification. They typically have red, orange, or yellow flowers; spicy or warming properties when tasted; or grow in hot, sunny environments. Chili peppers, with their intense heat, represent Fire's transformative intensity. Sunflowers, following the sun's path, channel solar Fire energy.

St. John's Wort, traditionally harvested at midsummer when Fire energy peaks, captures the light and warmth of the sun. Fire plants power workings for protection, courage, sexuality, motivation, and dramatic change.

Water plants enhance emotional awareness, intuition, dreams, healing, and love. These often grow in or near water; have high moisture content; or possess flowing, flexible structures. Seaweeds, directly harvested from the ocean, carry Water's depths and mysteries. Willow, thriving beside streams and ponds, embodies Water's flexible resilience. Cucumber, comprised mostly of water, cools and soothes like gentle rain. Water plants support magic involving emotional healing, psychic development, reconciliation, cleansing, and accessing the subconscious.

Many plants embody combinations of elemental energies, reflecting the complexity of the natural world. Rose carries both the emotional depth of Water in its associations with love and the passionate intensity of Fire in its traditional red color. Rosemary combines the mental clarity of Air with the protective qualities of Fire. These multi-elemental plants prove particularly versatile in magical formulations, bridging different energetic needs within a single working.

Understanding elemental plant associations allows practitioners to create balanced magical workings or to emphasize particular elemental qualities. A protection spell might incorporate predominantly Fire plants for active warding but include Earth elements for stability and grounding. A healing formula might balance Water plants for emotional repair with Earth plants for physical regeneration. Recognizing when a magical working—or the practitioner themselves—lacks elemental balance allows for corrective formulations that restore energetic equilibrium.

The elemental framework also helps witches attune to seasonal energies, as the elements traditionally correlate with the annual cycle. Spring associates with Air, summer with Fire, autumn with Water, and winter with Earth (though some traditions vary these assignments). By working with plants that embody the current seasonal element, practitioners align their magic with natural energetic tides, increasing potency and effectiveness.

PLANETARY AND ASTROLOGICAL CORRESPONDENCES

Planetary correspondences offer the most structured and detailed system for understanding plant energetics within Western magical traditions. This framework associates plants with the seven classical planets—Sun, Moon, Mercury, Venus, Mars, Jupiter, and Saturn—each representing specific energetic qualities and magical domains. Some expanded systems include the outer planets (Uranus, Neptune, Pluto) and fixed stars, but the classical seven provide the foundation for most herbal magical work.

Solar herbs radiate confidence, vitality, success, and illumination. These plants often have yellow flowers, follow the sun's movement, or reach upward with bright blooms. Sunflower, marigold, St. John's wort, and calendula exemplify solar energy. They strengthen magical workings for career advancement, recognition, health restoration, and truth-revealing. These herbs work best harvested at noon or during the sun's strongest presence, particularly near the summer solstice when solar power peaks.

Lunar herbs connect to intuition, dreams, emotions, cycles, and the unconscious. White-flowering night-bloomers like jasmine and moonflower directly embody lunar energy, as do water plants and those with round, moon-like leaves or fruits. Mugwort, renowned for enhancing dreams, carries particularly strong lunar properties. These plants enhance divination, psychic work, emotional healing, and fertility magic. They respond to moon phases, with their properties shifting subtly as the moon waxes and wanes—most potent for collection during the full moon when their psychoactive compounds often peak.

Mercury plants facilitate communication, learning, travel, and adaptability. These often have many small flowers, seeds capable of widespread distribution, or delicate, quickly-moving leaves. Fennel, lavender, marjoram, and dill fall under Mercury's influence. They excel in spells for enhancing mental abilities, successful negotiations, safe journeys, and overcoming obstacles through cleverness rather than force. These herbs work best harvested during Mercury hours (astrologically determined periods when Mercury's influence predominates) and respond well to Mercury retrograde periods for introspective or revisionary magical work.

Venus herbs attract love, pleasure, beauty, harmony, and artistic inspiration. Plants with sweet fragrances, soft textures, pink or red flowers, or heart-shaped leaves typically associate with Venus. Rose, hibiscus, vanilla, and apple blossom exemplify Venusian energy. They strengthen workings for all forms of love, sensuality, reconciliation, and aesthetic enhancement. Venus plants respond particularly well to Friday harvesting (Venus's day) and morning dew collection, which traditionally preserves their beauty-enhancing properties.

Mars plants provide courage, strength, protection, and passionate energy. These often have thorns, red coloration, spicy tastes, or other assertive characteristics. Dragon's blood, nettle, chili, and blackthorn demonstrate Martial qualities. They empower protective barriers, courage-building rituals, physical strength enhancement, and breaking through obstacles. Mars herbs work best harvested on Tuesday (Mars's day) during Mars hours, particularly when the planet is prominently placed in the night sky.

Jupiter herbs bring expansion, prosperity, generosity, and spiritual growth. These plants often produce abundant fruits, grow to impressive sizes, or possess dignified, stately qualities. Oak, nutmeg, sage, and maple exemplify Jupiterian energies. They excel in workings for wealth, opportunity, legal success, and wisdom development. Jupiter plants respond well to Thursday harvesting (Jupiter's day) during periods of abundance, particularly when collecting parts that demonstrate generosity, such as nuts or fruits.

Saturn plants connect to boundaries, discipline, longevity, and ancestral wisdom. These typically grow slowly, produce hard seeds or wood, or survive harsh conditions. Cypress, comfrey, yew, and patchouli carry Saturnian energy. They strengthen magical work involving protection, binding, establishing boundaries, and connecting to ancient knowledge. Saturn herbs work best harvested on Saturday (Saturn's day), particularly during winter months when Saturn's qualities of limitation and structure predominate in nature.

Traditional astrological timing enhances the effectiveness of plant harvesting and magical preparation. The planetary hour system divides daylight and nighttime into twelve divisions each, with hours varying in length according to seasonal daylight changes. Each hour falls under the dominion of a particular planet, creating optimal times for harvesting plants associated with that planetary energy. Similarly, the day of the week (each associated with a planet in traditional astrology) influences plant potency for its corresponding planetary herbs.

Moon phases provide another crucial timing consideration, particularly for plants with strong lunar associations. The waxing moon (new to full) generally supports magic involving increase, growth, and attraction, making it ideal for harvesting plants used in these applications. The waning moon (full to new) supports decrease, banishing, and release, appropriate for plants used in these functions. The quarter and cross-quarter days (solstices, equinoxes, and points between) offer particularly potent harvesting times for plants associated with seasonal transitions and elemental forces.

The zodiacal position of the sun and moon creates additional correspondences. Plants harvested when the moon occupies the sign governing a particular body part gain efficacy for healing that area—herbs collected during a Taurus moon, for instance, work particularly well for throat concerns, while an Aries moon strengthens herbs for head-related issues. Similarly, sun-ruled plants harvested when the sun transits Leo (its ruling sign) gain amplified potency for solar magical applications.

In practical application, these three systems—Signatures, Elements, and Planets—work best when used in complementary fashion. A plant like dandelion reveals its magical nature through multiple frameworks: its solar signature (yellow flower resembling the sun), its elemental association (primarily Air through its windborne seeds, with Earth aspects in its deep taproot), and its planetary correspondence (primarily Jupiter in its abundant growth with solar aspects in its appearance). Understanding these overlapping energetic qualities allows the witch to select precisely the right plant for each magical need and to combine herbs into effective, harmonious formulations.

By studying and working with these traditional frameworks while developing personal relationships with plants, the green witch builds a comprehensive understanding of plant energetics that bridges ancient wisdom and personal gnosis. This multilayered knowledge transforms simple botanical awareness into the sophisticated energetic understanding necessary for effective magical herbalism.

CHAPTER 3

CULTIVATING MAGICAL RELATIONSHIPS WITH PLANTS

Moving beyond theoretical frameworks, this chapter focuses on developing practical, living connections with plant allies. True herbal magic emerges not from books alone but through direct engagement with the plant world. By creating sacred growing spaces, communicating with plant consciousness, and practicing ethical harvesting, witches establish reciprocal relationships that form the core of authentic plant magic. These relationships transform plants from mere ingredients into true magical partners, enhancing both the efficacy of spellwork and the spiritual depth of one's practice.

CREATING A WITCH'S GARDEN

The witch's garden serves as both a physical space for growing magical herbs and a sacred boundary where intentional relationship with plants begins. Whether you tend a sprawling rural garden, a modest suburban plot, a collection of containers on an urban balcony, or simply a few potted herbs on a windowsill, the principles remain consistent: intentional design, energetic alignment, and regular magical engagement with your growing allies.

Planning a magical garden begins with honest assessment of your available space, growing conditions, and commitment level. Even the smallest growing space can produce powerful magic when maintained with consistent intention. Window boxes can support sun-loving protection herbs like rosemary and thyme. A single pot might nurture a relationship with magical basil for prosperity work. North-facing apartments with minimal direct light can host shade-tolerant magical allies like mint, sweet woodruff, or ferns. The witch's garden adapts to circumstances rather than demanding ideal conditions.

For those with outdoor growing space, consider organizing plants according to magical purpose, creating distinct areas dedicated to specific intentions. A protection garden near the entrance might include thorny blackberry, protective rosemary, and boundary-defining mugwort. A healing section could gather comfrey, plantain, calendula, and other medicinal allies. A visionary garden might host dream-enhancing plants like mugwort, damiana, and evening primrose. This organizational approach creates magical microclimates that amplify specific energetic intentions while making harvest more intuitive.

Alternatively, organize by elemental or planetary correspondences, grouping plants that share magical affinities. A Fire garden section featuring sun-loving, protective plants creates a concentrated pocket of transformative energy. A Venus garden bed gathering roses, strawberries, and other love-attracting plants generates a powerful resource for relationship magic. These magical groupings allow plants to communicate with each other, creating synergistic energy fields that exceed the power of isolated specimens.

When selecting plants for magical gardens, balance traditional correspondences with local adaptation. While classical magical herbs like rosemary and mugwort offer tested efficacy, native plants indigenous to your region often provide equal or greater magical potency with better ecological appropriateness. Research the magical properties of local flora or develop relationships with native plants to discover their magical affinities. These local magical allies typically require less intervention to thrive while connecting your practice more deeply to your specific bioregion.

Timing garden activities according to astronomical and seasonal influences significantly enhances magical efficacy. Planting during the waxing moon supports vigorous growth, particularly for herbs harvested for their leaves and flowers. The waning moon better supports root development, ideal for herbs valued for their underground parts. The moon's astrological sign further refines timing—planting during a Cancer moon enhances emotional properties, while an Aries moon strengthens protective qualities.

Seasonal timing provides broader magical context. Spring planting aligns with new beginnings and fresh manifestations.

Summer maintenance work supports abundance and fullness. Fall harvesting connects to preservation and preparation for inward journeys. Winter garden planning facilitates deep dreaming and vision work for the coming growth cycle. By aligning garden activities with these natural rhythms, the witch harmonizes personal magical practice with universal energetic tides.

The physical act of preparing soil becomes a magical ritual in itself. As you amend earth with compost, speak intentions for growth and transformation. When turning soil, visualize releasing obstacles to magical manifestation. Each practical gardening task offers opportunity for magical alignment when approached mindfully. These simple workings infuse the growing space with consistent magical intention before seeds or plants even arrive.

Magical garden maintenance extends beyond physical care to include regular energetic tending. Moon water irrigation during appropriate lunar phases enhances plant magical properties. Singing or chanting to plants during morning watering establishes communication pathways. Mindful weeding—distinguishing between unwanted plants and volunteer allies—develops discernment while maintaining appropriate boundaries. These practices transform routine garden maintenance into ongoing relationship-building with plant allies.

Dedicated garden altars further enhance the magical nature of growing spaces. These can be elaborate or minimalist—a simple stone at the garden entrance acknowledges the space's sacred nature, while more complex arrangements might include specific elemental representations, seasonal decorations, and offerings for plant allies. The altar serves as a focal point for garden blessings, a place to express gratitude for harvests, and a physical reminder of the garden's magical purpose.

Even those without traditional garden access can create magical growing relationships. Sprouts grown on kitchen countertops provide rapid magical allies for urgent needs. Foraged relationships with plants in public parks offer alternatives to cultivation. Participation in community gardens provides growing space while creating connections with human and plant communities simultaneously. The witch's garden exists wherever intentional relationship with plants occurs, regardless of conventional definitions of gardening space.

COMMUNICATION AND CONNECTION WITH PLANT SPIRITS

Beyond physical cultivation lies the more subtle art of establishing communication with plant consciousness. This practice fundamentally shifts the witch's relationship with herbs from utilitarian usage to collaborative partnership. While initially challenging for those accustomed to viewing plants as objects rather than beings, developing these communication skills transforms magical practice, providing clearer guidance for appropriate plant applications and significantly enhancing magical efficacy.

The first step in plant communication involves recognizing plants as conscious entities with their own intelligence, rather than passive objects. This represents a profound perspective shift for many raised in cultures that deny plant consciousness. Scientific research increasingly supports what magical practitioners have always known—plants demonstrate complex responses to their environments, communicate with each other through mycorrhizal networks, remember past conditions, and adapt behaviors based on experience. This growing scientific validation helps skeptical practitioners open to the possibility of meaningful communication with plant intelligence.

Begin developing communication skills through regular meditation with specific plant allies. Start with plants already familiar in your environment—garden herbs, houseplants, or prominent trees in your neighborhood. Approach the plant with respect, presenting yourself honestly and clearly stating your intention to communicate. Regular visits establish familiarity, with plants gradually recognizing your energy and becoming more responsive over time. This slow, consistent approach respects the different temporal experience of plant consciousness, which operates on cycles different from human immediacy.

Simple listening meditation forms the foundation of plant communication. Sit comfortably with a plant and quiet your mind through breath focus. When sufficiently centered, expand your awareness to include the plant's presence. Instead of projecting questions immediately, simply remain receptive to impressions, emotions, physical sensations, or images that arise. These subtle responses may initially seem like imagination but gradually reveal patterns that constitute the plant's communication style. Journal these experiences to track developing patterns in communication.

As communication pathways strengthen, experiment with more direct exchanges. Mentally pose simple questions and remain open to responses, which typically arrive as intuitive knowing, symbolic images, or physical sensations rather than human language. Begin with basic inquiries about the plant's needs or preferences regarding water, light, or position. These practical questions provide clear feedback loops—if you receive an impression the plant needs more water, follow through and observe results. These verification opportunities build confidence in your reception abilities.

Dream work offers another pathway for deeper plant communication. Before sleep, place a leaf from a plant ally under your pillow or a living plant near your bed, requesting dream communication. Keep a journal beside your bed to record impressions immediately upon waking. Plant communications in dreams often use rich symbolism that reveals deeper aspects of the plant's magical affinities and specific applications for your practice. These dream relationships develop over time into profound magical alliances that significantly enhance waking communication.

Advanced practitioners develop communication through carefully approached plant journeys using mild preparations of appropriate visionary herbs. These traditional practices require extensive preparation, mentorship, and ritual safeguards. When approached with appropriate respect and protection, these experiences can provide direct transmission of plant knowledge that dramatically accelerates understanding of herbal magical properties. However, these practices should never be undertaken casually or without proper guidance.

For all practitioners, regardless of experience level, developing plant communication requires rigorous discernment. Distinguish between actual plant communication and your own projections or fantasies. Verify information received through research, experimentation, and consultation with experienced herbalists. Approach communication with sincere respect rather than demanding immediate responses. Most importantly, maintain ethical reciprocity—listening to plants includes respecting when they decline participation in magical workings.

ETHICAL WILDCRAFTING PRACTICES

While garden relationships form the foundation of many magical practices, wildcrafting—the harvesting of plants from their natural habitats—offers connection to herbs unavailable in cultivation and attunement to the full power of plants growing in their chosen environments. However, with habitat destruction and overharvesting threatening many magical species, ethical considerations must guide wildcrafting practice. Responsible wildcrafting balances the witch's need for magical allies with broader ecological responsibilities and appropriate cultural respect.

The fundamental principle guiding ethical wildcrafting is reciprocity. Never approach wild harvesting as merely taking; instead, conceptualize it as an exchange relationship. For every plant harvested, something should be returned to the ecosystem and the plant community. This reciprocity takes many forms: physical offerings, removal of invasive species, habitat protection activities, seed dispersal efforts, or dedicated magical workings benefiting the land. This exchange acknowledges the gift represented by each harvested plant and maintains balanced relationship with the ecosystem.

Before harvesting, develop familiarity with relevant regulations and land status. Public lands operate under various jurisdictions with different harvesting rules—national forests, state parks, wildlife management areas, and other designations carry specific legal restrictions. Private lands require explicit permission from landowners. Some areas prohibit harvesting entirely, while others require permits or limit collection quantities. Responsible wildcrafters research and respect these legal frameworks, recognizing they often (though not always) serve important conservation purposes.

Species identification represents both a practical and ethical requirement. Mistaken identification can result in harvesting rare protected species, damaging ecosystems, or collecting potentially harmful plants. Develop relationships with experienced botanists, join local plant walks, invest in region-specific field guides, and practice identification skills regularly. Never harvest when uncertain of identification, and document unfamiliar plants with photographs for later research rather than collecting specimens. This cautious approach prevents unintentional harm through misidentification.

Population assessment precedes any harvest. Observe the

abundance of the target species in the specific location and broader region. Count individual plants in the immediate area and estimate what percentage would be affected by your harvest. Consider whether the plant is common locally but rare regionally or globally. Check conservation resources like local rare plant lists, IUCN Red List status, or United Plant Savers' Species At-Risk list. This thorough assessment determines whether harvesting remains appropriate or should be reconsidered.

When harvesting proves appropriate, follow quantity guidelines that maintain plant populations. Never harvest more than 10% of a plant population in a given area—for smaller populations or slower-growing species, reduce this percentage further. For individual perennial plants, take no more than 25% of the plant material, allowing sufficient resources for recovery. For roots and other harvest that destroys individual plants, ensure abundant population size and limit collection to no more than 5% of mature specimens. These conservative limits prioritize ecosystem integrity over individual needs.

Timing harvests according to plant life cycles demonstrates respect while maximizing magical potency. Harvest leaves before flowering when their energy concentrates in foliage. Collect flowers at peak bloom but before seed formation begins. Gather seeds after full ripening but before natural dispersal. Dig roots during dormant seasons when plants store energy underground. These timing considerations support both ecological sustainability and magical efficacy, aligning practical and spiritual considerations.

Harvesting technique directly impacts plant survival and regeneration. Use sharp, clean tools to make precise cuts that heal efficiently. For branches and stems, cut at appropriate angles that shed water and resist infection. When collecting roots, take only a portion of larger root systems when possible, re-covering disturbed areas thoroughly. Harvest in ways that encourage rather than diminish future growth, such as pruning stimulating bushier growth in many species. These mindful techniques reduce harvest impact while supporting continued plant vitality.

Beyond physical harvesting practices, magical intention and acknowledgment play crucial roles in ethical wildcrafting. Before harvesting, communicate your intentions to both individual plants and the broader ecosystem. Request permission through meditation or direct communication practices, remaining genuinely open to refusal. Express specific gratitude for each plant harvested, acknowledging its sacrifice. Leave appropriate offerings based on research, cultural context, and personal relationship with the land. These spiritual practices complete the reciprocity cycle while deepening magical connection to harvested plants.

Cultural considerations add another essential ethical dimension. Many traditional magical plants hold sacred status for indigenous communities with ongoing cultural relationships to these species. Research whether plants you intend to harvest have specific cultural significance, particularly for indigenous peoples of your region. When such significance exists, consider whether your harvest might impact access for practitioners from these traditions. Seek education about appropriate approaches from practitioners within relevant cultural traditions when possible, while respecting boundaries around sacred knowledge not intended for sharing. These considerations prevent unintentional participation in extractive appropriation of cultural plant relationships.

Transportation and processing continue ethical practice beyond the harvest moment. Prepare beforehand with appropriate containers that maintain plant freshness and integrity. Process harvested plants promptly and respectfully, acknowledging their transition from living beings to magical allies through appropriate rituals. Maintain mindfulness throughout processing, recognizing that ethical relationship extends beyond the harvest moment to encompass the plant's full journey into magical application.

Finally, documentation completes the ethical wildcrafting cycle. Record harvest locations, quantities, observations about plant populations, and magical intentions in your grimoire or harvesting journal. This practice creates accountability, allows monitoring of harvest impacts over time, and builds a personal database of sustainable practices specific to your bioregion. Detailed documentation also preserves the context of the plant's origin, maintaining connection to place as an aspect of the plant's magical properties.

Through these ethical wildcrafting practices, the green witch becomes not merely a harvester of magical materials but a conscious participant in ecological relationships and magical lineages. This approach transforms wildcrafting from potential exploitation into a practice that can actively benefit plant communities while providing powerful allies for magical work. The most advanced practitioners find that ethical harvesting itself becomes a powerful magical act—one that aligns personal intention with broader ecological harmony, enhancing the potency of all subsequent magical applications.

By intentionally cultivating magical gardens, developing genuine communication with plant intelligence, and practicing ethical wildcrafting, witches establish authentic relationships with the plant kingdom. These living connections transform herbs from mere magical ingredients into true allies and teachers. The effort invested in building these relationships returns manifold power to magical practice, creating workings grounded in reciprocity, respect, and genuine connection to the green world.

CHAPTER 4

THE MAGICAL APOTHECARY: ESSENTIAL HERBS

Having established the theoretical foundations of herbal magic and developed relationships with plant allies, we now turn to the practical heart of the green witch's craft: the magical apothecary. This carefully curated collection of herbs forms the physical foundation of effective magical practice. While an experienced witch may work with hundreds of botanical allies throughout their lifetime, this chapter focuses on essential herbs that address fundamental magical needs: protection, healing, and manifestation. These core categories represent the most frequent applications of herbal magic and provide the foundation upon which more specialized workings can later be built.

PROTECTIVE HERBS FOR MAGICAL SAFETY

Protection represents the most fundamental application of herbal magic and the appropriate starting point for any practitioner. Before exploring other magical realms or attempting complex workings, establishing effective protection ensures both physical and energetic safety. Protective herbs create boundaries between helpful and harmful energies, shield practitioners during vulnerable magical operations, and cleanse spaces of unwanted influences. These botanical guardians have stood watch over witches' workings for millennia, their protective properties verified through generations of practical experience.

Rosemary (Rosmarinus officinalis) stands as perhaps the most versatile protective herb in the Western magical tradition. Its sharp, cleansing aroma cuts through negative energy, while its sturdy, needle-like leaves symbolize impenetrable barriers. Beyond general protection, rosemary specifically guards against energy theft and magical manipulation. Hang dried branches over doorways to prevent negative influences from entering. Burn as incense during divination to protect against misleading spirits. Add to ritual baths before undertaking challenging magical work. Rosemary's protective properties combine with excellent preservation qualities, making it an ideal herb to incorporate into long-lasting protective amulets and sachets.

Rue (Ruta graveolens), often called "herb of grace," provides particularly potent protection against hexes and intentionally directed negative energy. Its bitter properties in both taste and energy repel magical attacks while strengthening personal boundaries. Rue's distinctive blue-green foliage contains compounds that can cause photosensitivity and skin irritation, a physical manifestation of its spiritual boundary-enforcing properties. Use with appropriate caution—its powerful protective qualities come with proportional potential for irritation when mishandled. Incorporate small amounts into protective sachets, especially when dealing with known magical conflicts. Plant near the home entrance to prevent negative energy from crossing your threshold. Add to floor washes for thorough energetic cleansing after psychic disturbances.

Blackthorn (Prunus spinosa) embodies protective fierceness through its formidable thorns and astringent fruits. Associated with warrior energy and defensive magic, blackthorn has historically protected against both physical and spiritual threats. Its thorns represent piercing discernment that identifies approaching danger, while its slow growth symbolizes the development of mature protection systems that function reliably under pressure. Carry a carefully prepared blackthorn protective charm during confrontational situations. Place thorns (mindfully harvested with appropriate protection) at property boundaries to establish energetic perimeters. Use the wood for crafting protective wands particularly suited for defensive magic and establishing firm boundaries.

Agrimony (Agrimonia eupatoria) provides subtle but effective protection particularly suited for empaths and sensitives who regularly encounter challenging energies through their work. Unlike harsher protective herbs that create impenetrable barriers, agrimony allows appropriate energetic exchange while filtering out harmful influences—ideal for healers, counselors, or those who must remain open while still maintaining protection. Its sunny yellow flowers belie its powerful protective qualities, demonstrating that effective protection need not always present as forbidding or harsh. Carry in protective sachets during situations requiring emotional openness combined with energetic safety. Prepare as an infusion to sprinkle around spaces used for healing work. Add to protection blends when full sensory awareness must be maintained during magical operations.

Angelica (Angelica archangelica) brings the protective quality of spiritual guardianship, specifically shielding against negative entities and unwanted spiritual attachments. As its name suggests, angelica has traditional associations with angelic protection in Western magical traditions, though similar protective properties appear in various cultural understandings of this powerful plant. Its sweet aroma masks substantial protective strength, making it particularly effective in situations requiring protective power with a gentle presentation. Use root pieces in protective amulets worn during spirit communication. Burn dried stalks as protective incense during channeling or mediumship. Plant near windows and doors to prevent intrusion by unwanted energies.

Protective herbal magic extends beyond individual plants to synergistic combinations addressing specific protective needs. For protection during sleep and dreamwork, combine mugwort, lavender, and a small amount of rosemary in dream pillows. For sanctuary creation within your home, develop a custom incense blend from protective herbs aligned with your specific needs and spiritual background. For maintenance of long-term protective boundaries, create a series of matched sachets to place at entryways, refreshing their contents seasonally to maintain active protection.

Application methods significantly impact protective efficacy. Smoke cleansing with appropriate protective herbs provides rapid intervention during acute situations, the smoke reaching areas difficult to access through other methods. Herbal washes offer thorough cleansing for spaces with lingering negative energy, the water element adding fluidity that reaches into corners and crevices. Protective sachets placed strategically throughout a space create an interconnected network of protection points, particularly effective for maintaining ongoing boundaries. Protective plant allies grown around the perimeter of your property establish living guardianship that strengthens over time as plants mature and establish deeper roots.

Regular protective maintenance prevents minor energetic disturbances from developing into significant problems. Establish seasonal protection rituals aligned with natural cycles—major cleansing at winter's end to remove stagnant energy, boundary reinforcement at summer's height when energetic activity peaks, and protective harvesting during fall's preparations for winter introspection. These rhythmic protective practices become integral aspects of the green witch's magical housekeeping, maintaining energetic hygiene alongside practical care of magical tools and spaces.

HERBS FOR HEALING AND WELLNESS MAGIC

Healing magic represents one of humanity's oldest applications of herbal knowledge—the boundary between medicinal and magical use of plants for healing appears only in relatively recent history. Today's green witch recognizes that effective herbal healing often operates simultaneously on physical, emotional, and spiritual levels. This holistic approach acknowledges the interconnection between these aspects of being and utilizes herbs capable of addressing multiple dimensions of healing simultaneously.

Lemon balm (Melissa officinalis) serves as a primary healing ally for emotional balance and heart healing. Its gentle yet effective action soothes anxiety, lifts mild depression, and mends emotional wounds without causing further disruption to sensitive systems. The plant's natural affinity for bees (reflected in its genus name Melissa, meaning "bee" in Greek) connects to its ability to bring sweetness back into lives experiencing emotional difficulty. Prepare as tea during times of emotional distress or heartbreak. Create an infused honey to slowly dissolve emotional barriers. Include in healing sachets placed near the heart during sleep to facilitate emotional processing. Lemon balm's magical healing properties complement its clinically studied anxiolytic effects, demonstrating how magical and medicinal properties often align.

Calendula (Calendula officinalis) excels in healing

magic addressing physical wounds, inflammation, and boundary restoration. Its sunny flowers promote tissue regeneration while simultaneously working on energetic levels to repair tears in the subtle body caused by trauma, surgery, or energetic attacks. The plant's notable ability to self-seed and flourish with minimal care reflects its magical property of supporting the body's inherent healing capabilities. Infuse in oils for application to physical wounds along with appropriate magical intention. Add dried petals to healing baths after experiences that have left spiritual or emotional wounding. Place fresh flowers on altars dedicated to healing work, replenishing with new blooms throughout the healing process to maintain momentum.

Yarrow (Achillea millefolium) stands as one of the most ancient and respected healing herbs, with archaeological evidence of its use dating back over 60,000 years. Its primary magical healing affinity involves boundaries—both in the literal sense of stopping bleeding and in the energetic sense of restoring appropriate boundaries after violation or depletion. The plant's feathery, divided leaves symbolize its ability to address complex healing needs with precise, tailored energy. Carry as an amulet during recovery from situations involving boundary violations. Use in healing baths following energy depletion from empathic overextension. Incorporate into magical workings designed to staunch energetic leaks or heal spiritual wounds affecting the energetic body's integrity.

Rose (Rosa spp.) bridges physical and emotional healing through its affinity for the heart in all its aspects. Different rose varieties offer subtle variations in healing energy, from the fierce protection of wild roses to the gentle nurturing of damask varieties, allowing practitioners to select precisely the right healing quality needed. Beyond its well-known association with romantic love, rose facilitates deeper healing of the spiritual heart's capacity for compassion, forgiveness, and authentic connection. Create rose petal elixirs for healing grief and heartbreak. Use rose water for cleansing ritual objects between emotional healing sessions. Incorporate petals into healing sachets designed to mend trust after betrayal. The rose's combination of beauty and thorns reminds us that complete heart healing includes both vulnerability and appropriate protection.

Comfrey (Symphytum officinale), traditionally called "knitbone," excels in magical healing work involving structural repair, both physical and energetic. Its remarkable ability to speed bone and tissue healing extends metaphysically to repairing foundational damage in one's energetic structure and life path. Comfrey's deep tap root represents its ability to access and heal issues with distant origins or deep unconscious roots. Create healing compresses for application to areas needing structural support during both physical healing and corresponding energetic repair. Plant near healing spaces to support recovery from trauma affecting one's foundational sense of safety. Use in magical workings designed to reconnect fragmented aspects of self following severe disruption to identity or purpose.

Effective healing magic often requires addressing overlapping needs through carefully designed herbal combinations. For grief processing that has manifested as physical symptoms, combine rose for heart healing, linden for emotional vulnerability, and comfrey for structural support. For recovery from prolonged stress that has depleted multiple systems, create a formula including lemon balm for nervous system support, ashwagandha for adrenal restoration, and lavender for sleep healing. For magical support during major medical interventions, develop protective-healing combinations featuring yarrow for boundary maintenance, calendula for wound healing, and rosemary for protection against opportunistic energy drains during vulnerability.

Timing significantly impacts healing efficacy. Acute situations benefit from immediate, intensive application, while chronic conditions require sustained, rhythmic support. Moon phases provide natural timing frameworks—begin healing work addressing excessive conditions during the waning moon, while deficiency states respond better to waxing moon energy. Align long-term healing work with appropriate seasonal energy; spring supports initiating growth of new healthy patterns, while autumn facilitates release of conditions no longer serving wellness.

Intention-setting creates the essential magical dimension of herbal healing work. Before preparing any healing formula, clarify precisely what healing outcome you seek, being specific about both physical and energetic aspects of the desired healing. Ground this intention in realistic understanding of natural healing processes and timeframes. Connect this specific intention to broader wellness context, recognizing how the immediate healing need relates to overall balance. Incorporate this clarified intention directly into each stage of preparation through visualization, verbal affirmation, or ritual gestures appropriate to your tradition.

The green witch approaches healing magic with appropriate humility and care. Magical healing supports but rarely replaces appropriate medical care for serious conditions. The most effective healing witches maintain productive relationships with conventional healthcare providers, recognizing the complementary strengths of different healing modalities. This integrated approach honors both the ancient wisdom of herbal healing traditions and contemporary medical knowledge, creating a comprehensive healing framework that addresses all aspects of well-being.

MANIFESTATION AND PROSPERITY PLANTS

While protection secures and healing restores, manifestation magic actively shapes reality according to intention. Prosperity represents one of the most common manifestation categories, addressing not only financial abundance but the broader concept of thriving in all life areas. Herbs with manifestation affinities help align intention with action, remove blocks to natural abundance, and create energetic conditions that support desired outcomes.

Basil (Ocimum basilicum) serves as a primary herb for general prosperity and abundance magic. Its rapid growth from tiny seeds to lush, abundant plants mirrors the expansion of prosperity from small beginnings. Beyond strictly financial applications, basil supports overall life abundance—relationships, opportunities, creativity, and joy. The plant's association with both luxury (its name derives from "royal" or "kingly") and everyday nourishment makes it particularly effective for balanced prosperity that enriches life without creating excess or greed. Place potted basil in kitchens and workspaces to attract steady abundance. Add leaves to prosperity sachets carried during job interviews or business negotiations. Incorporate into money-drawing floor washes for businesses or home offices. Basil's versatility in magical applications matches its culinary adaptability, making it an accessible prosperity ally for practitioners at all experience levels.

Cinnamon (Cinnamomum verum) accelerates manifestation through its warming, activating energy that overcomes stagnation and resistance. Its sweet-spicy nature specifically addresses prosperity blockages stemming from beliefs about unworthiness or scarcity consciousness, helping to transform these limiting patterns into receptivity to abundance. Sprinkle powdered cinnamon at thresholds to invite prosperous visitors and opportunities. Add cinnamon sticks to prosperity candles to accelerate manifesting fire. Incorporate into sachets designed to overcome financial inertia or remove blocks to deserved recognition. Cinnamon's intense aroma serves as an effective magical intensifier, strengthening the focus and energy behind prosperity intentions.

Allspice (Pimenta dioica) brings the magical property of multiplication, taking existing prosperity and expanding it through its radiating warmth. Unlike herbs that attract new prosperity, allspice specifically enhances and preserves current resources, making it particularly valuable during times of consolidation or when building upon existing success. The berries contain the magical signatures of multiple spices (hence the name "allspice"), reflecting their capacity to develop multiple prosperity streams from single sources. Add to money-drawing sachets focused on investment growth rather than new income. Use in prosperity magic designed to extend the usefulness or value of existing resources. Incorporate into workings intended to expand successful ventures into new markets or applications. Allspice works best in magical formulas after initial prosperity has been established, functioning as a magical prosperity multiplier.

Mint (Mentha spp.) excels in prosperity magic related to quick money, unexpected windfalls, and financial agility. Its rapid growth habit and tendency to spread reflects its magical affinity for creating prosperity that arrives through surprising channels and expands through creative adaptation. Different mint varieties carry subtle variations in prosperity energy—peppermint bringing clarity to financial decisions, spearmint attracting quick cash, and apple mint drawing steady, sustainable increases. Add to wallets or purses to attract unexpected income. Place in cash registers to increase business. Use in road-opening workings to create new financial pathways. Mint's association with both luxury and practical household use makes it particularly effective for manifesting prosperity that bridges everyday needs and special abundance.

High John the Conqueror root (Ipomoea jalapa) brings the magical property of overcoming obstacles to prosperity, particularly those involving power imbalances, systemic barriers, or seemingly insurmountable challenges. This powerful prosperity ally originated in African American conjure traditions but has become widely adopted in various magical systems for its remarkable effectiveness in demanding prosperity situations. Carry as a personal charm during challenging negotiations or when facing significant financial hurdles. Add to prosperity workings when external barriers rather than internal blocks limit abundance flow. Incorporate into blessing oils for anointing tools used in business or professional advancement. High John's intense determination energy supports prosperity acquisition requiring persistence and strategic action rather than passive attraction.

Bay laurel (Laurus nobilis) lends prosperity magic the qualities of recognition, victory, and achievement—appropriate for manifestation work focused on career advancement, public acknowledgment, or competitive success. Its historical association with crowning victors and honoring achievements connects directly to prosperity arising from excellence and merit rather than random chance. Place bay leaves inscribed with specific career goals under altar candles during manifestation rituals. Add dried leaves to sachets carried during performances, competitions, or job interviews. Burn as incense before important presentations or when launching creative projects. Bay enhances prosperity magic particularly for those whose abundance flows through recognized expertise or creative excellence.

Manifestation work requires careful preparation beyond herb selection. Before beginning prosperity magic, articulate precisely what form of abundance you seek—random cash, steady income flow, recognition leading to advancement, resources for specific projects, or general increase in life abundance. This clarity prevents the common magical pitfall of manifesting prosperity in unexpected or undesirable forms. Examine whether internal blocks or limiting beliefs may interfere with prosperity reception, addressing these through appropriate magical work before attempting direct manifestation. Ensure willingness to receive through appropriate channels, recognizing that prosperity often arrives through unexpected avenues requiring flexibility and openness.

Application methods for prosperity magic involve both symptomatic (creating desired outcomes) and symbolic (representing prosperity states) approaches. Money-drawing floor washes blend practical cleaning with energetic opening to prosperity. Prosperity gardens featuring abundance-associated herbs create living magical engines that continuously generate wealth-attracting energy. Cash box herbs placed with currency attract similar energy, while wallet sachets carried on the person create continuous prosperity fields. Prosperity candles dressed with appropriate herbal oils concentrate intention through focused flame. These diverse application methods allow practitioners to maintain consistent prosperity work through multiple complementary approaches.

Ethical considerations hold particular importance in prosperity magic. The green witch recognizes that true abundance operates through circulation rather than hoarding, designing prosperity workings that benefit communities rather than depleting shared resources. Manifestation intentions include appropriate compensation for value received rather than seeking unearned gains. Prosperity magic functions best when aligned with practical action, magical work supporting rather than replacing effective financial practices. These ethical foundations prevent prosperity magic from becoming merely materialism dressed in spiritual language, instead creating authentic abundance that enriches both practitioner and community.

Through thoughtful work with these protective, healing, and manifestation herbs, the green witch builds a magical apothecary addressing fundamental magical needs. As practice develops, this core collection expands to include more specialized allies for particular magical applications. The herbs described here provide not merely ingredients but relationships with plant allies whose proven magical affinities have supported practitioners through generations of magical work. By developing your own connections with these essential magical herbs, you establish the foundation for a lifetime of effective herbal magic practice.

CHAPTER 5

ADVANCED HERBAL CORRESPONDENCES

Having established a foundation with essential herbs, we now explore more specialized botanical allies organized by their physical structure and magical function. This chapter examines three major categories of advanced herbal correspondences: trees and woods, underground plants, and the reproductive parts of plants (flowers, seeds, and fruits). Understanding these specialized plant parts and their unique magical properties allows the witch to select precisely the right botanical ally for specific magical purposes, creating more nuanced and effective workings.

MAGICAL PROPERTIES OF TREES AND WOODS

Trees represent some of our oldest and most powerful magical allies, their size, longevity, and presence making them natural repositories of significant magical energy. Working with trees, whether through direct communion with living specimens or through the use of their wood, bark, and other products, connects practitioners to deeply rooted magical currents and enduring natural power.

Oak (Quercus spp.) stands as perhaps the most venerated magical tree across numerous European traditions. Its impressive longevity and size embody endurance, protection, and strength. Magically, oak carries the energy of steadfastness, helping to establish permanence in magical workings intended to create lasting change. The tree's ability to withstand lightning strikes connects it to sky powers and divine authority, making it an effective intermediary between earthly and celestial realms. Oak's acorns carry concentrated manifestation energy—potential futures contained in compact form. Work with oak for protection magic requiring substantial, long-term shields rather than quick fixes. Use oak wood for crafting altars that need to hold and stabilize significant magical energy. Carry acorns during new ventures to support steady growth and successful manifestation. Approach living oak trees for communion with ancient wisdom and support during major life transitions requiring inner strength.

Willow (Salix spp.) embodies flexibility, intuition, and connection to water energies. Its association with the moon and feminine mysteries makes it particularly effective for divination, dreamwork, and emotional healing. Willow's ability to root from cuttings reflects its magical property of establishing new growth from challenging circumstances. Unlike oak's rigid strength, willow teaches the magical wisdom of bending without breaking—the strength found in adaptability rather than resistance. Use willow branches for crafting divination wands, especially those used near water or during moon rituals. Carry willow bark for emotional healing following grief or heartbreak. Sit beneath living willows when seeking guidance about situations requiring adaptability or when needing to connect with unconscious wisdom. Willow excels in magic involving transition states, making it particularly useful during initiations or life passages requiring surrender to transformation.

Pine (Pinus spp.) carries magical properties of purification, prosperity, and vitality even through dark times. Its evergreen nature represents constancy and life-force maintained during periods of dormancy or challenge. Pine's abundant resin contains concentrated magical energy for protection, particularly against psychic attack and negative entities. The tree's towering, straight growth pattern carries energy of direct action and clear intention. Burn pine needles for space purification when more traditional herbs like sage are unavailable or inappropriate. Use pine resin in protective amulets, particularly those designed to maintain boundaries against subtle intrusions. Craft ritual tools from pine wood when working with prosperity magic, especially for maintaining abundance through challenging cycles. Pine's continuous growth pattern makes it particularly effective for magical work spanning extended periods, supporting consistent progress toward distant goals.

Hawthorn (Crataegus spp.) specializes in threshold magic, governing boundaries between worlds and states of being. Its spring blooming and fall fruiting connect it to both life and death energies, making it a powerful ally for working with ancestral connections and communication between realms. Hawthorn's impressive thorns provide protection specifically against malevolent spirits and unwanted otherworldly influences. The tree's traditional association with the fairy realm makes it a potent intermediary for communication with nature spirits and elemental forces. Use hawthorn wood for crafting pendulums or divination tools designed to access hidden information. Plant hawthorn at property boundaries for protection against negative spiritual influences while still allowing positive energies to flow freely. Work with hawthorn flowers for opening psychic abilities, and with berries for grounding and integrating spiritual experiences. Approach hawthorn with particular respect, acknowledging its ancient associations with otherworldly powers and its protective function at liminal spaces.

Rowan (Sorbus aucuparia) serves primarily as a powerful protective ally, especially against enchantment, deception, and magical manipulation. Its bright red berries symbolize alertness and vigilance, while its compound leaves represent complexity and discernment. Rowan's traditional placement near doorways across Northern European traditions speaks to its effectiveness as a threshold guardian. Unlike more aggressive protective trees, rowan specifically protects against subtle magical intrusions while still allowing beneficial energies to flow freely. Carry rowan berries for protection against manipulation and mind-influencing magic. Plant rowan near home entrances to prevent harmful energies from entering while welcoming beneficial visitors. Craft protective amulets from rowan wood, particularly for those who work with potentially deceptive spiritual forces. Rowan provides especially appropriate protection for diviners, mediums, and those whose magical work requires psychic openness, as it guards against deception without blocking genuine spiritual communication.

Working with tree spirits differs from interaction with smaller herbs, requiring adjusted approaches and expectations. Trees operate on different time scales than humans or smaller plants, their communication often slower and more deliberate but carrying greater depth and perspective. Approach tree work with patience, allowing relationships to develop gradually through repeated visits and consistent presence. Begin communication with respectful introduction and clear statement of intention, recognizing the tree as an autonomous being with its own purposes and preferences. Offerings appropriate for tree spirits include water (especially during dry periods), song, organic mulch, or careful removal of invasive species threatening the tree's health. Through these respectful practices, profound relationships with tree spirits develop over time, providing protection, teaching, and magical partnership of extraordinary power.

Wood from different trees carries distinct magical properties even after separation from the living tree. For crafting ritual tools, match wood type to magical purpose—oak for stability and grounding, cherry for love and compassion work, ash for communication between worlds. The directional orientation of the wood within the living tree affects its magical properties—branches reaching toward the sky carry uplifting energy appropriate for wands, while root wood maintains grounding properties ideal for altar bases. Season wood appropriately before magical use, recognizing that proper drying preserves magical properties while preventing future cracking or warping of finished tools. When harvesting wood directly, do so with explicit permission from both the tree spirit and legal authorities, taking only what falls naturally whenever possible. These mindful practices maintain respectful relationship with tree allies while creating effective wooden tools that carry the specific magical properties of their source trees.

MAGICAL USES OF ROOTS AND UNDERGROUND PLANTS

Below the earth's surface lies a hidden realm of profound magical significance. Root systems, bulbs, rhizomes, and tubers operate in darkness, drawing nourishment directly from soil and establishing foundational support for visible growth above. Working with these underground plant parts connects practitioners to chthonic energies, ancestral wisdom, and the deep, hidden aspects of magical transformation.

Angelica root (Angelica archangelica) provides powerful protection with specific affinity for warding against malevolent spiritual entities. Unlike the aerial parts of the plant, which offer more generalized protective energy, the root contains concentrated protective power specifically attuned to establishing and maintaining boundaries against intrusive spirits. This protection extends to dreamwork and psychic activities, making angelica root valuable for practitioners who regularly engage with spirit realms. Carry pieces of dried root as protective amulets during spiritual communication work. Burn small amounts with protective intention to clear spaces after negative entity encounters. Add to protective baths before undertaking communication with potentially challenging spiritual beings. The root's sweet yet commanding energy creates protection that remains permeable to beneficial spiritual exchanges while firmly excluding negative influences.

Ginger (Zingiber officinale) rhizome accelerates magical processes through its warming, activating energy. Unlike many roots that stabilize and ground, ginger specifically speeds manifestation, breaks through stagnation, and energizes magical workings that have stalled or slowed. This acceleration applies particularly to prosperity magic, spell reversals, and workings requiring swift change rather than gradual transformation. Add small pieces to spell bottles when immediate results are needed. Incorporate into incense blends for rituals designed to overcome obstacles or resistance. Use in magical workings performed during waning moon phases to accelerate the release of unwanted conditions or blockages. Ginger's fiery nature in both taste and magical effect makes it especially effective for quick, decisive magical actions rather than subtle, gradual change.

Mandrake (Mandragora officinarum) root historically represents one of the most potent magical allies for fertility, love-drawing, and profound transformation. Its anthropomorphic appearance—often resembling human form—connects it to ancient traditions viewing this plant as semi-human, capable of mediating between human needs and natural forces. Though true mandrake remains rare and endangered, related plants in the Nightshade family (particularly American mandrake or mayapple) carry similar though less concentrated magical properties. Work with mandrake root for sex magic and fertility rituals with appropriate ethical boundaries. Use in dream pillows for prophetic dreaming, particularly regarding major life transitions. Incorporate with extreme caution and appropriate protection into magical workings involving significant personal transformation. Mandrake's powerful nature demands experienced handling and clear boundaries, making it inappropriate for beginning practitioners.

Dandelion root (Taraxacum officinale) offers magical properties of divination, psychic communication, and summoning. Its remarkable ability to break through seemingly impenetrable surfaces—growing through concrete and asphalt—translates magically into the ability to access hidden information and overcome barriers to communication. Unlike more dramatic divinatory allies, dandelion provides clear, practical insights rather than overwhelming visions. Harvest roots during the waning moon for workings involving breaking through obstacles. Prepare as elixir for enhancing psychic abilities in practical applications such as finding lost objects or accessing forgotten information. Incorporate into dream pillows for clear guidance dreams free from excessive symbolism or confusion. Dandelion's common presence makes it an accessible ally for developing divinatory abilities without working with more toxic or restricted visionary plants.

Orris root (Iris florentina) excels in magic involving love, mediation, and communication between seemingly incompatible energies. While the iris flower symbolizes messenger energy between worlds, the root specifically grounds these communications into material reality. This translating function makes orris particularly valuable for clarifying magical intentions and ensuring they manifest as desired rather than through misinterpreted alternate forms. Add to sachets designed to attract compatible romantic partners rather than merely temporary attractions. Incorporate into communication-enhancing spell work, particularly for resolving long-standing misunderstandings. Use in magical workings requiring clear transmission of intentions to spirits or elemental forces. Orris root's subtle bridging energy makes it especially appropriate for complex magical workings where precision of communication significantly impacts outcomes.

Working with underground plant parts requires specific magical considerations beyond those for aerial herbs. Roots magically connect to stability, foundation, nourishment, and hidden aspects of any situation or working. Their growth in darkness links them to unconscious processes, making them particularly effective for magic addressing deep-seated patterns or accessing unconscious knowledge. Harvesting roots generally kills or significantly damages the plant, creating greater ethical responsibility for ensuring necessity and sustainability. These factors make magical root work both potent and carrying significant responsibility, demanding clear intention and ethical harvesting practices.

Appropriate harvesting times for magical root collection generally differ from those for aerial parts. Many roots reach peak magical potency during plant dormancy, when energy concentrates below ground—typically late fall after aboveground portions have died back, or early spring before new growth emerges. Moon phase significantly impacts root properties, with the waning moon supporting magical functions involving banishing, binding, or accessing hidden knowledge. The dark moon specifically enhances root magic addressing the deepest, most concealed aspects of situations. These timing considerations significantly impact magical effectiveness when working with underground plant parts.

FLOWERS, SEEDS, AND FRUITS IN MAGIC

The reproductive parts of plants—flowers, seeds, and fruits—embody transformative energy, generative power, and magical potential. These plant parts represent the culmination of the plant's life cycle, containing concentrated life force and future possibility. Working with these generative plant portions connects practitioners to manifestation, fruition, and the fulfillment of magical intention.

Rose flowers (Rosa spp.) carry perhaps the most complex and nuanced magical properties among flowering plants. Beyond their well-known association with romantic love, different rose varieties and colors access distinct magical energies—red roses for passionate love, white for spiritual illumination, pink for gentle healing, yellow for mental clarity, and wild roses for protective boundaries. The rose's structure—beautiful yet protected by thorns—embodies the magical wisdom of appropriate vulnerability balanced with necessary boundaries. Use in heart-healing rituals addressing emotional wounds while establishing healthier relationship patterns. Incorporate into self-love workings that balance genuine self-care with release of narcissistic tendencies. Create rose elixirs for attracting love relationships that offer both authentic intimacy and appropriate independence. Rose magic particularly excels in nuanced emotional workings requiring balance between seemingly opposed qualities rather than simplistic manifestation of single emotional states.

Sunflower (Helianthus annuus) combines solar energy with remarkable manifestation properties through both its flowers and seeds. The flower's sun-following behavior connects it directly to solar magical currents of vitality, visibility, and confident authority. Its impressive growth from small seed to towering stalk embodies manifestation of potential into substantial reality. Use flowers in magic designed to increase personal presence and recognition in professional settings. Incorporate seeds into prosperity workings, particularly those involving expansion from small beginnings. Place sunflowers on altars during summer rituals celebrating achievement and abundance. The plant's combination of impressive height and sturdy structure makes it particularly effective for magic involving sustained success rather than brief recognition.

Evening primrose flowers (Oenothera biennis)

specialize in magical timing, transition moments, and liminal states. Their dramatic evening blooming—flowers opening within minutes at dusk—connects them to threshold magic and moments of sudden transformation. Unlike more gradual magical allies, evening primrose facilitates abrupt shifts in consciousness, sudden insight, and rapid transition between states of being. Harvest flowers at the moment of opening for workings involving initiation or step-changes in spiritual development. Use in dream enhancement preparations, particularly for lucid dreaming and conscious dreamwork. Incorporate into rituals performed at twilight when seeking to access in-between states or communicate between worlds. Evening primrose particularly supports magical transformations requiring precise timing and readiness to seize momentary opportunities for significant change.

Pomegranate fruit (Punica granatum) carries powerful magical associations with abundance, fertility, and the underworld across numerous cultural traditions. Its multiple seeds contained within a single fruit represent magical multiplication of resources and opportunities. The fruit's association with underworld journeys (most famously through the Persephone myth) connects it to transformative experiences involving symbolic death and rebirth. Split pomegranates open during prosperity rituals to symbolize and attract abundance that emerges from hidden sources. Use seeds in fertility magic of all kinds—creative projects, business ventures, and traditional fertility when appropriate. Incorporate into magical workings involving conscious engagement with shadow aspects or personal underworld journeys. Pomegranate's combination of sweet and bitter flavors makes it particularly appropriate for magical work acknowledging that significant rewards often require navigating challenging passages.

Poppy seeds (Papaver spp.) facilitate visionary experiences, dreamwork, and access to the collective unconscious. Unlike working with more potent parts of the plant, the seeds provide gentler access to altered awareness without overwhelming consciousness. Their numerous tiny form represents the multiple entry points to unconscious wisdom, while their traditional use in sleep-inducing preparations connects them to dream magic. Incorporate into dream pillows for prophetic dreaming with appropriate protective boundaries. Use in divinatory preparations when seeking access to ancestral wisdom or cultural memory. Add to incense blends for rituals involving controlled journeying between ordinary and non-ordinary consciousness. Poppy seed magic requires clear intention and boundaries to prevent ungrounded experiences or spiritual untethering.

Working effectively with flowers requires understanding their ephemeral yet powerful nature. Flowers represent the peak of the plant's expressive energy—their fragrance, color, and form embody the essence of the plant's magical properties in concentrated form. This concentration makes fresh flowers particularly potent for immediate magical workings, while proper preservation techniques allow extended access to their properties. Harvest flowers at their energetic peak—typically mid-morning after dew has dried but before hot sun diminishes essential oils. Many flowers reach magical potency slightly before full opening, capturing the anticipatory energy of potential just before full expression. These timing considerations maximize the magical properties available for both immediate use and preservation.

Seeds contain remarkable magical significance as vessels of complete potential in miniature form. Every seed contains the entire future plant in latent form, making seeds powerful magical allies for potential, possibility, and carefully directed intention. Their dormant state represents patience and proper timing—the understanding that manifestation occurs when conditions properly align rather than through forced growth. Use seeds in long-term spell work designed to manifest gradually with natural timing. Incorporate into intention-setting rituals at project beginnings. Plant specific magical seeds with clear intention, allowing their growth to parallel and support the manifestation of your magical goals. Seed magic teaches the essential magical wisdom of planting with clear intention and then providing appropriate conditions for natural development rather than attempting to force premature results.

Fruits embody the principle of magical fulfillment—the manifestation of flower potential into nourishing form. Their ripening process parallels magical manifestation, transforming initial intention through gradual development into mature expression. Different fruit forms carry specific magical signatures—berries bring concentrated magical potency in small packages; drupes with their central stones represent essential truth surrounded by sweeter accessible wisdom; pomes embody the principle of protected core knowledge surrounded by accessible teachings. Use fruits in rituals celebrating accomplishment and magical fulfillment. Incorporate into gratitude practices acknowledging successful manifestations. Share magically charged fruits to distribute specific magical influences through communal consumption. Fruit magic particularly supports abundance work that recognizes and celebrates sufficiency rather than endless accumulation.

Working with these advanced herbal correspondences—trees and woods, underground plants, and reproductive plant parts—expands the witch's magical vocabulary beyond basic herbs into more specialized and nuanced botanical relationships. These plant allies offer precise magical energies for specific purposes, allowing for increasingly sophisticated and effective magical workings. As you develop relationships with these botanical categories, your herbal magic will gain both greater subtlety and heightened potency, accessing the full spectrum of plant magical possibilities.

CHAPTER 6
CREATING MAGICAL HERBAL PREPARATIONS

Transforming raw botanical materials into effective magical tools requires both technical skill and magical awareness. This chapter explores the practical craft of creating magical herbal preparations, covering three essential categories: preservation methods, liquid extractions, and dry preparations. These techniques form the foundation of the green witch's laboratory practice, allowing practitioners to capture, preserve, and enhance the magical properties of plant allies for diverse magical applications.

DRYING AND STORING MAGICAL HERBS

The art of properly preserving herbs represents perhaps the most fundamental skill in herbal magic. Effective drying and storage techniques maintain both the physical and magical properties of plants, allowing their energy to remain accessible long after harvest. Without proper preservation, even the most potently harvested herbs quickly lose their efficacy, rendering subsequent magical applications ineffective. Understanding the principles and practices of herbal preservation ensures that your carefully cultivated and ethically wildcrafted plants remain magically potent throughout their useful life.

Timing significantly impacts preservation success. The magical potency of most herbs peaks at specific points in their growth cycle—flowers typically reach maximum potency just as they fully open, leaves generally contain highest concentration of both essential oils and magical properties just before flowering begins, while roots typically concentrate their energy during plant dormancy. Harvesting at these optimal times provides the strongest starting material for preservation. Beyond growth stage, consider environmental conditions—harvest aerial parts on dry mornings after dew has evaporated but before hot sun diminishes essential oils; collect roots during appropriate moon phases to align with their magical purpose.

Immediate post-harvest handling directly affects magical potency retention. Process herbs promptly after collection to prevent deterioration of volatile compounds that often carry significant magical properties. Remove damaged portions, which can accelerate deterioration of the entire batch. For leafy herbs and flowers, avoid washing unless absolutely necessary, as water contact can diminish essential oils and accelerate decomposition. When washing proves unavoidable, use quick rinses and thorough drying methods. These immediate care practices preserve maximum magical potency before formal preservation begins.

Drying methods should align with each herb's specific structure and constituent properties. Aerial herbs with delicate flowers or high essential oil content benefit from hanging in small bundles in dark, well-ventilated spaces where gentle air circulation preserves color and aromatic compounds. Thick, juicy herbs require faster drying methods to prevent mold development—single-layer placement on screens or dehydrators set at low temperatures (below 95°F/35°C) prevent spoilage while preserving magical properties. Roots typically require cleaning, slicing to appropriate thickness for even drying, and slightly higher temperatures to penetrate their denser tissues. Throughout any drying process, maintain consciousness of the herb's magical identity through verbal acknowledgment, sigils placed in drying areas, or other practices that maintain magical connection during this transitional stage.

Technique: Preserving Magical Potency in Lavender
Materials Needed:
- Freshly harvested lavender stalks with flowers
- Cotton string or unbleached twine
- Scissors
- Dark paper bags (optional)
- Labels and permanent marker
- Dedicated drying space

Magical Timing: Harvest lavender on a waning moon

morning when flowers are fully formed but not yet fully open, preferably during Venus or Mercury hours for love or communication magic respectively.

Preparation Steps:

1 Harvest lavender stalks just as the first flowers open but before full bloom, cutting at least 6 inches below the flower head.

2 Gather stalks in small bundles of 8-12 stems, arranging them so flower heads align.

3 Tie stems securely with cotton string, creating a loop for hanging.

4 As you tie each bundle, speak your intention: "Lavender of peace and protection, retain your power in this preservation."

5 Hang bundles upside down in a dark, dry space with good air circulation, away from direct sunlight.

6 For highest essential oil retention, place paper bags around flower heads with holes punched for ventilation.

7 Check after 1-2 weeks; properly dried lavender should retain color but feel crisp to touch, with stems that snap rather than bend.

8 Once dried, strip flowers from stems and store in airtight glass containers labeled with harvest date, location, and magical intention.

Magical Storage Enhancement: Place a small piece of clear quartz in each storage jar to maintain lavender's energetic properties. On each full moon, place closed jars in moonlight for several hours to recharge their protective and calming properties.

Storage containers significantly impact herb longevity and magical integrity. Glass jars with tight-fitting lids provide ideal vessels for most dried herbs, preventing moisture absorption while allowing visual monitoring for quality changes. Amber or cobalt glass offers additional protection against light degradation for particularly light-sensitive herbs. Label all containers with not only herb name but harvest date, location, and specific magical intention, creating complete magical documentation for each preserved herb. Store containers in cool, dark locations—traditional herb cabinets or dedicated shelves away from heat sources, sunlight, and moisture. This physical protection extends the magical lifetime of preserved herbs significantly.

Organizational systems enhance both practical access and magical focus. Arrange stored herbs according to categories meaningful to your practice—by magical purpose (protection, healing, divination), by plant family relationships, by elemental or planetary correspondence, or by frequency of use. Whatever system you choose, maintain it consistently, allowing intuitive access during magical need while preventing degradation from excessive handling during searches. Consider creating dedicated storage spaces for herbs with particularly powerful or potentially incompatible energies, preventing cross-contamination between protective and attracting herbs or between banishing and manifesting allies. This thoughtful organization creates a magical apothecary that functions as a coherent magical tool rather than mere ingredient storage.

Regular inventory assessment protects against using herbs

past their magical prime. Most dried leaves and flowers maintain optimal magical properties for approximately one year, while roots, barks, and berries may retain potency for two to three years when properly stored. Beyond physical degradation signs (color fading, aroma loss, texture changes), assess magical potency through direct handling, pendulum testing, or other divination methods appropriate to your practice. Ritually released expired herbs through conscious composting with gratitude, returning their physical form to the earth while acknowledging their service. This regular cycling maintains the vitality of your magical apothecary while demonstrating respect for the life energy of your plant allies.

HERBAL OILS, TINCTURES, AND EXTRACTS

Liquid herbal preparations capture and concentrate plant properties in forms that facilitate diverse magical applications. These preparations extract specific plant constituents through appropriate solvents—oils, alcohol, vinegar, or water—creating potent magical tools that combine the properties of both herb and medium. Understanding how to create these liquid preparations expands the witch's magical repertoire significantly, offering applications impossible with dry herbs alone.

Herbal oils serve as primary vehicles for topical magical applications, ritual anointing, and candle dressing. Two major preparation methods offer different magical properties—cold infusion maintains delicate energetic qualities through gentle extraction, while hot infusion accesses deeper, more stubborn plant constituents through heat application. Cold infusions generally work best for flowers, leaves, and other delicate plant parts carrying volatile magical energies, while hot infusions better suit roots, barks, and resins requiring more forceful extraction. The base oil selected contributes its own magical properties to the final preparation—olive oil for protection and blessing, almond oil for healing and prosperity, coconut oil for purification and spiritual connection. This combination of herb and oil properties creates a synergistic magical tool greater than either component alone.

Technique: Solar-Infused St. John's Wort Oil for Confidence Magic

Materials Needed:
- Fresh St. John's Wort flowers and top leaves
- High-quality olive oil
- Clean, dry glass jar with tight-fitting lid
- Cheesecloth and straining container
- Dark glass bottle for storage
- Label materials

Magical Timing: Harvest St. John's Wort at its magical peak—around the summer solstice when flowering begins, ideally at noon during a waxing moon for maximum solar energy.

Preparation Steps:

1 Gather flowers and top few inches of the plant in late morning after dew has dried but before midday heat.
2 Allow plant material to wilt slightly (4-6 hours) to reduce water content but preserve magical solar properties.
3 Fill your jar loosely with plant material to about 2/3 capacity.

4 Pour olive oil over herbs until completely covered with an additional inch of oil above plant material.
5 Stir with a wooden wand or stick dedicated to solar workings, moving in a clockwise direction while visualizing radiant golden light entering the mixture.
6 Seal jar tightly and label with herb name, date, and magical intention: "Solar Confidence and Inner Light."
7 Place in a sunny window or sheltered outdoor location where it will receive direct sunlight for at least 4 hours daily.
8 Shake gently each day at noon, reinforcing the solar connection with an affirmation such as: "By the power of the sun, confidence and clarity come."
9 After 2-4 weeks (a complete moon cycle is ideal), the oil should develop a rich red color, indicating successful extraction.
10 Strain through cheesecloth into your storage bottle, squeezing to extract all oil.
11 Store in a dark glass bottle in a cool, dark place.
Magical Usage: Anoint solar plexus before confidence-requiring events, dress yellow or gold candles for personal empowerment rituals, or apply to petition papers for job interviews or performance situations.

Alcohol-based tinctures extract and preserve both water-soluble and alcohol-soluble plant constituents, creating concentrated magical preparations with extended shelf life. Traditional magical practice often employs high-proof clear spirits like vodka or grain alcohol, though brandy or whiskey may be selected when their specific magical properties complement the herb being tinctured. Tinctures excel at capturing and preserving the magical properties of fresh herbs that lose significant potency when dried—especially those with subtle psychoactive or visionary properties. Beyond preservation benefits, the alcohol itself acts as a magical catalyst, activating and amplifying the herb's properties while providing a vehicle that quickly enters the bloodstream when internal consumption proves appropriate. These preparations become particularly valuable for dream work, altered consciousness rituals, or magical operations requiring rapid onset of herbal magical properties.

Vinegar extractions provide acid-based solutions that extract different plant constituents than alcohol or oil, particularly mineral components with grounding and protective magical properties. Apple cider vinegar brings additional properties of healing and harmony, while white vinegar carries stronger banishing and cleansing energies. These preparations excel at magical household applications—floor washes for magical home protection, cleansing sprays for ritual objects, or purification baths for energetic clearing. The sharp odor of vinegar itself contributes boundary-defining and negative-energy-repelling properties to these preparations, making them particularly effective for space clearing and protection work.

Water-based preparations—including infusions (teas), decoctions, and hydrosols—utilize water's receptive qualities and universal solvent properties for magical applications requiring fluidity, adaptability, and emotional connection. Hot water infusions excel at extracting delicate magical properties from leaves and flowers for immediate ritual use, while decoctions use prolonged simmering to access the deeper magical properties of roots, barks, and berries. Hydrosols or flower waters capture the volatile essential oils and subtle energetic imprints of plants through steam distillation, creating gentle magical waters particularly suited for emotional and spiritual applications. Water's inherent magical properties of purification, emotional resonance, and intuitive connection enhance these preparations, making them especially effective for scrying, dream work, emotional healing, and intuitive development.

Moon-infused waters represent specialized water preparations charged through direct lunar exposure. Different moon phases imbue these waters with specific magical properties—new moon water for beginnings and renewal, full moon water for culmination and maximum power, waning moon water for banishing and release work. These lunar waters become potent magical tools both independently and as bases for other preparations. Use full moon water as the base for prosperity-enhancing herbal infusions, new moon water for intention-setting ritual baths, or dark moon water for scrying and divination work. The combination of specific lunar energy with appropriate herbal allies creates powerful magical tools aligned with lunar cycles.

POWDERS, INCENSE, AND SMOKING BLENDS

Dry herbal preparations provide some of the most versatile and portable magical tools available to the green witch. These preparations concentrate herbal properties into forms that can be easily transported, applied in precise amounts, or activated through specific elements—particularly fire for incense and smoking blends. Understanding how to create effective dry preparations expands the practitioner's magical versatility significantly, allowing adaptation to diverse ritual contexts and magical needs.

Herbal powders serve numerous magical functions from directly marking magical boundaries to inconspicuous application in everyday environments. Creating effective magical powders requires complete drying followed by careful grinding to consistent texture appropriate for the intended application—fine powders for subtle scattered applications, coarser grinds for visible boundary marking. Traditional grinding tools include dedicated mortars and pestles, with materials selected for magical correspondence—stone for grounding and permanence, wooden for growth and vitality, ceramic for transformation and refinement. During grinding, maintain focused intention on the powder's magical purpose, transforming mechanical action into magical act through consciousness. Store completed powders in containers appropriate to their magical purpose—glass for clarity and purity, metal for protection and strength, ceramic for transformation and manifestation.

Technique: Protection Powder for Home Boundaries
Materials Needed:
- 2 tablespoons dried rosemary (protection, purification)
- 2 tablespoons dried sage (cleansing, wisdom)

- 1 tablespoon dried black peppercorns (immediate protection, banishing)
- 1 tablespoon dried sea salt (purification, grounding)
- 1 teaspoon dried garlic granules (banishing, ward against negativity)
- Mortar and pestle (stone preferred)
- Dark glass container with tight-fitting lid
- Small piece of black tourmaline (optional)

Magical Timing: Create during the waning moon, preferably on Saturday (Saturn's day) during a planetary hour of Mars or Saturn for maximum protective strength.

Preparation Steps:

1 Cleanse your work area and tools with sage smoke or appropriate purification method.

2 Place black tourmaline in mortar if using, to amplify protective properties.

3 Add rosemary to mortar first, grinding while speaking: "By rosemary's strength, protection surrounds me."

4 Add sage, continuing to grind while stating: "By sage's wisdom, negativity is revealed and banished."

5 Add peppercorns, grinding forcefully while declaring: "By pepper's heat, immediate protection manifests."

6 Add salt, grinding while affirming: "By salt's purity, this space is cleansed and sealed."

7 Add garlic granules last, completing the blend with: "By garlic's power, all harmful intentions are turned away."

8 Continue grinding until mixture reaches uniform consistency—not too fine (so it can be seen when applied) but well integrated.

9 Transfer to container while visualizing a shield of protective blue-white light surrounding the powder.
10 Seal and label with name, date, and purpose: "Boundary Protection Powder."

Magical Usage:
• Sprinkle across thresholds of doors and windows while visualizing an impenetrable barrier forming.
• Create protective lines around property boundaries during waning moon phase.
• Add small amounts to the four corners of your home, reapplying after cleaning or during times of vulnerability.
• Sprinkle small amount in shoes before entering challenging situations for personal protection.

Incense crafting represents one of the oldest herbal magical arts, using fire to transform plant material into smoke that carries intentions between worlds. Various incense forms serve different magical purposes—loose incense burned on charcoal disks provides immediate and adjustable intensity; incense sticks or cones offer controlled, sustained burning for longer rituals; and combustible incense "ropes" or logs provide slow-releasing continuous effects for extended workings. Beyond primary herbs, incense formulations often include natural resins (frankincense, myrrh, copal) that function both as magical ingredients and binding agents. Combustion enhancers like saltpeter may be included in self-igniting preparations, though many traditional magical incense blends rely solely on natural flammability. The process of incense creation itself becomes ritual practice, with each ingredient added with specific intention, transforming mechanical formulation into magical act.

The aromatic smoke from properly prepared incense serves multifaceted magical functions. Purification represents perhaps the most universal application, with smoke cleansing spaces of unwanted energies while simultaneously consecrating them for magical work. Smoke also functions as a carrying medium, transporting prayers, intentions, and offerings to spirits, deities, or other realms of existence. The visible movement of incense smoke provides divinatory information, with traditional smoke reading interpreting patterns and directions as meaningful communication. For personal magical application, incense smoke readily adheres to auras and subtle bodies, carrying herbal magical properties into the practitioner's energetic field for lingering effect. These diverse applications make incense one of the most versatile and important herbal preparations in the witch's repertoire.

Smoking blends for direct inhalation represent a more controversial category of magical herbal preparation, with significant considerations regarding safety, legality, and appropriate use. Traditional magical traditions worldwide have employed ceremonial smoking of specific herbs for visionary purposes, spiritual communion, or energetic shifting. Contemporary practitioners must approach this category with extraordinary caution, thorough research, and clear ethical boundaries. Legal herbs with mild relaxing or focusing properties—mugwort, damiana, mullein—may be judiciously incorporated into personal practice where appropriate, while substances with significant psychoactive properties or legal restrictions remain outside ethical practice regardless of historical precedent. When exploring this traditional category, prioritize safety through thorough research, start with minimal quantities of well-documented herbs, and maintain clear consciousness regarding the significant difference between ceremonial use and recreational consumption.

Beyond these three major categories lie numerous specialized herbal preparations with specific magical applications. Bath herbs and salts provide immersive magical experiences combining water's receptivity with herbal properties. Floor washes blend practical cleaning with magical intention for space purification and blessing. Herbal pillows and dream sachets facilitate dream magic and sleep protection. Exploring these diverse preparation methods expands your magical repertoire while deepening relationship with herbal allies through varied interactions and applications.

Throughout all herbal preparation, maintain consciousness that you create not merely physical products but magical tools imbued with intention, relationship, and power. The quality of attention during preparation directly affects magical efficacy—distracted, mechanical production yields weak tools, while mindful, intentional creation produces potent magical allies. This consciousness transforms simple herbal crafting into true magical laboratory work, where each preparation becomes both an expression of relationship with plant allies and a focused magical operation in itself.

CHAPTER 7

HERBAL TOOLS AND TALISMANS

The transformation of herbs into dedicated magical tools and talismans represents an advanced application of herbal magic, bridging the realms of herbalism, enchantment, and craft. This chapter explores three primary categories of herbal tools: portable charm bags and sachets, wooden ritual implements, and living plant guardians. These creations extend herbal magic beyond temporary applications into enduring magical allies that provide ongoing support and protection. By crafting these herbal tools, the witch creates a network of botanical partnerships that continuously emanate specific magical influences into their environment and magical practice.

CRAFTING HERBAL CHARM BAGS AND SACHETS

Herbal charm bags—also known as sachets, medicine pouches, mojo bags, or spell bundles—represent one of the most versatile and portable forms of herbal magic. These compact tools concentrate specific herbal energies into forms that can be carried on the person, placed in strategic locations, or gifted to others in need of particular magical support. Their inconspicuous nature allows for continuous magical work even in settings where overt magical practice might be inappropriate, making them essential tools for the contemporary witch navigating diverse environments.

The effectiveness of charm bags stems from the concentrated combination of appropriately selected herbs, focused intention, and proper activation. Unlike temporary herbal applications that disperse their energy quickly, charm bags provide sustained magical influence through contained herbal blends that continue emanating their properties over extended periods. This persistent magical presence makes them particularly valuable for ongoing needs like protection during travel, sustained confidence in challenging work environments, or continuous attraction of specific opportunities.

Design considerations begin with clarity about the specific magical intention. Successful charm bags address focused, specific needs rather than vague or overly broad purposes. A bag designed for "protection during air travel" will prove more effective than one for "general safety," while a sachet for "attracting new clients to my healing practice" will work more efficiently than one for "general prosperity." This specificity guides all subsequent choices from herb selection to container material to activation method.

Herbal selection forms the core of effective charm bag creation. Begin with a foundation herb that aligns most directly with your primary intention—rosemary for protection, lavender for peace, cinnamon for quick energy. Add complementary herbs that support secondary aspects of your purpose—perhaps adding rose to a protection blend to ensure the protection comes through love rather than fear, or adding sage to a prosperity mix to ensure wealth arrives with wisdom in its use. Consider including personal connection items when appropriate—a strand of hair for self-directed magic, a written name for work targeting others (with appropriate consent), or a tiny image representing the desired outcome.

Recipe: Travel Protection Charm
Magical Purpose: Creates a portable protection against travel hazards, delays, and negative energies encountered while journeying.

Materials:
- Small drawstring bag (blue or black fabric for protection)
- 1 tablespoon rosemary (protection, mental clarity)
- 1 tablespoon cedar chips (protection, particularly during movement)
- 1 teaspoon black salt (absorbs negative energy)
- 3 bay leaves (protection, especially against unexpected threats)
- 1 small piece of jet or black tourmaline (grounding, protection)

- 1 small piece of paper with your name and birthdate
- Red thread for binding
- White candle for activation

Timing: Create during the waxing moon for enduring protection, ideally on Thursday (Jupiter's day) for protection during expansion and journeys.

Assembly Instructions:

1 Cleanse all materials through your preferred method (smoke, moonlight, sound).

2 Write your name and birthdate on the small paper, then add the phrase: "I journey in safety, protected on all paths."

3 Fold the paper toward you three times while visualizing yourself surrounded by protective blue light.

4 Place rosemary in the bag first, stating: "By rosemary's shield, I am protected from all harm."

5 Add cedar chips, stating: "By cedar's strength, my journey remains smooth and secure."

6 Add black salt, stating: "By salt's purity, negativity is absorbed before reaching me."

7 Add bay leaves one by one, stating: "By bay's wisdom, dangers become visible before they affect me."

8 Add your personal paper, stating: "This protection is specifically for me, (your name), on all my travels."

9 Add the protective stone last, stating: "By earth's endurance, this protection remains strong throughout my journey."

10 Pull the drawstring closed and bind with red thread, wrapping it three times and tying three knots.

Activation:

1 Hold the completed charm bag between your palms, generating warmth.

2 Pass the bag through the smoke of protective incense or herbs if available.

3 Light a white candle and circle the bag around the flame three times clockwise, saying: "With fire's light, this charm activates. With herb's might, this protection permeates. Alert and aware, safe and sound, Protection follows me, wherever I'm bound."

4 Carry the charm in your luggage, vehicle, or pocket while traveling.

Maintenance: Squeeze the bag between your hands before each trip to reactivate. Refresh every six months by opening, adding a drop of protective essential oil (cedarwood or rosemary), and resealing with renewed intention.

Container selection should align with both practical needs and magical purpose. Natural fabric containers—cotton, linen, silk, or wool—allow herbal energies to emanate while containing physical material. Color choices enhance magical intention: red for vitality and protection, blue for peace and healing, green for growth and prosperity, purple for spiritual development, black for absorption of negativity. Size balances practical portability with sufficient space for effective herbal combinations. For charm bags meant to be carried continuously, durability becomes essential—double-stitched seams and secure closures prevent accidental spilling and magical disruption.

Activation methods transform assembled materials from

potential to actualized magical tools. Fire activation—passing the completed bag through candle flame or incense smoke—infuses quick, transformative energy. Water activation—sprinkling with moon water or appropriate magical waters—adds fluidity and emotional connection. Personal energy activation—breathing into the bag while visualizing its purpose, sleeping with it under your pillow for three nights, or carrying it against your skin for a full day—creates direct energetic links between practitioner and tool. Many traditional practices combine multiple activation methods for comprehensive empowerment.

Maintenance ensures continued effectiveness over time. Unlike single-use spells, charm bags require periodic refreshing to maintain optimal function. Reactivation through original methods refreshes energy when potency diminishes. Physical refreshing—adding drops of appropriate essential oils, exposing to moonlight or sunlight aligned with the bag's purpose, or periodically adding small amounts of fresh herbs—maintains material connections. Set regular maintenance schedules based on usage intensity—bags carried daily might need monthly refreshing, while those placed statically in homes might require attention only at seasonal transitions or major life changes.

Ethical disposal acknowledges the magical nature of these tools when their purpose completes or effectiveness ends. Biodegradable components can be ritually returned to earth with gratitude, preferably at appropriate locations—protection herbs at boundaries, prosperity herbs near home foundations, healing herbs near water sources. Non-biodegradable components receive cleansing before repurposing or respectful disposal. This conscious completion honors the magical relationship established with the herbal allies while properly closing the energetic circuit created during the charm's active life.

CRAFTING HERBAL WANDS, STAFFS, AND RITUAL TOOLS

Wooden ritual tools with herbal origins represent some of the most enduring and powerful implements in the witch's arsenal. Unlike ephemeral preparations, these solid tools embody the living essence of trees and shrubs transformed into focused magical conduits. Creating these implements connects practitioners to ancient magical traditions while developing intimate relationships with specific tree allies whose qualities become integral to the witch's practice.

Wood selection forms the foundation of effective tool creation, with each tree species offering distinct magical properties. Oak provides stability, strength, and enduring protection, ideal for primary wands and altars requiring substantial grounding energy. Willow brings flexibility, intuition, and emotional healing, perfect for divination tools and implements used in grief work or emotional magic. Rowan offers powerful protection specifically against enchantment and deception, valuable for tools used in truth-seeking or counter-magic. Elder brings the liminal energy of thresholds between worlds, suited for spirit communication and ancestral work. Hazel facilitates wisdom, communication, and knowledge-seeking, excellent for teaching wands and divination tools. This thoughtful matching of wood type to magical purpose creates tools with inherent affinity for their intended magical applications.

Harvesting practices significantly impact tool efficacy. Traditional harvesting involves requesting permission from both the tree itself and the land's spirits or owners. Many traditions recommend harvesting only fallen branches whenever possible, minimizing harm while working with wood the tree has willingly released. When direct cutting proves necessary, proper timing enhances magical properties—harvesting during appropriate moon phases, planetary hours, or seasonal transitions aligned with the tool's intended purpose. Offering thanks and appropriate gifts—water, organic mulch, songs, or magical workings benefiting the tree's community—completes the honorable exchange. These respectful harvesting practices establish positive relationship with the tree ally from the beginning of tool creation.

Technique: Crafting a Rowan Protection Wand
Magical Purpose: Creates a powerful tool for casting protective circles, directing defensive energy, and nullifying harmful magic directed at the practitioner or their space.
Materials:
• Rowan branch approximately 12-15 inches long and thumb-thickness
• Sharp knife dedicated to magical work
• Sandpaper (medium and fine grit)
• Natural oil for sealing (olive, jojoba, or almond)

- Red thread or ribbon
- Small protective crystals (black tourmaline, clear quartz, or jet)
- Protective herbs (rosemary, rue, or dragon's blood resin)
- Beeswax (optional for sealing)

Timing: Harvest rowan during the waning moon for protective purposes, ideally on Tuesday (Mars day) for defensive strength or Saturday (Saturn day) for boundary reinforcement.

Harvesting Protocol:

1 Approach a rowan tree respectfully, introducing yourself and your intention.

2 Present an offering (water, birdseed, or a song).

3 Request permission to take a branch, listening quietly for intuitive response.

4 If permission feels granted, thank the tree and select a healthy branch with minimal impact to the tree's growth.

5 Make a clean cut with your ritual knife, avoiding tearing or splintering.

6 Leave a second offering after harvesting in gratitude.

Crafting Process:

1 Allow the wood to cure for one full moon cycle in a dry, dark place.

2 Begin physical shaping during the waxing moon to infuse growing power.

3 Remove bark carefully, preserving it for later use in protective sachets.

4 Shape the wand with your knife, working slowly and with focused intention on its protective purpose.

5 Create a slight point at the directing end and a comfortable handle at the base.

6 Sand progressively smoother, beginning with medium and finishing with fine grit.

7 As you sand, chant or visualize protective energy building in the wood.

8 Create a small depression near the base to hold protective herbs.

9 Mix protective herbs with a few drops of beeswax or resin to form a small ball.

10 Press this mixture into the depression, sealing it with a wrapped binding of red thread.

Consecration:

1 Present the completed wand to each of the four elements:
- Pass through incense smoke (Air)
- Pass quickly through candle flame (Fire)
- Sprinkle with protective moon water (Water)
- Touch to salt or soil (Earth)

2 Anoint with protective oil while speaking your dedication: "Rowan of power, defender of old, Through your wood, protection unfolds. Ward against harm, shield against bane, Protect and defend in this tool you remain."

3 Wrap the wand in black or blue cloth and place on your altar for three nights to fully integrate its energies.

Usage Guidelines:

- Use to cast protective circles by pointing and directing energy clockwise.
- Trace protective symbols in the air to activate their power.
- Place on altars to maintain continuous protective presence.

• Touch to doors and windows while visualizing sealing them against negative influences.
• Store wrapped in its dedicated cloth when not in use.

Maintenance: Re-oil the wood quarterly to prevent drying. Refresh the protective herbs annually on the same date the wand was created. If the wand absorbs significant negative energy through defensive work, cleanse by passing through protective incense smoke or burying briefly in salt.

Physical crafting techniques transform raw wood into refined magical implements. Basic tool creation requires minimal equipment—a sharp knife, appropriate sandpapers, and finishing materials. Begin by removing bark unless specific magical purposes dictate its retention. Shape gradually and mindfully, allowing the wood's natural form to guide design while ensuring practical functionality. Sand progressively from coarse to fine grits, moving with the wood's grain to prevent splintering. Throughout physical shaping, maintain magical consciousness through chanting, visualization, or periodic ritual pauses to reconnect with the implement's intended purpose.

Embellishment options enhance both aesthetic appeal and magical function. Carving appropriate symbols directly into the wood creates permanent magical programming—protection sigils, planetary glyphs, elemental symbols, or personal magical marks align the tool with specific energetic currents. Crystal additions contribute complementary energies—clear quartz for amplification, amethyst for spiritual connection, black tourmaline for grounding and protection. Wrapped handles using appropriate colored threads, ribbons, or leather cords both improve grip and add corresponding color energies. Metal accents—copper for energy direction, silver for intuitive connection, gold for solar empowerment—can be incorporated as wire wrapping or inlaid pieces. These embellishments should enhance rather than distract from the wood's inherent properties, creating harmonious energy combinations rather than chaotic competing influences.

Consecration transforms crafted objects into true magical tools through ritual acknowledgment and energetic alignment. Elements often feature prominently in consecration—presenting the tool to air, fire, water, and earth in sequence acknowledges its participation in the complete manifest world. Anointing with appropriate oils seals the tool's purpose while providing physical protection for the wood. Naming the tool creates specific magical identity and facilitates deeper relationship. Many traditions include usage demonstration during consecration—casting a circle with a new wand, performing a divination with a new pendulum—establishing proper magical function from the beginning. These consecration practices formally transition the implement from crafted object to magical ally.

Proper care maintains both physical integrity and magical potency. Physical maintenance includes regular oiling to prevent drying and cracking, proper storage protecting from extreme temperatures and humidity, and periodic inspection for damage requiring repair. Magical maintenance involves cleansing after significant workings to remove accumulated energetic residue, recharging through exposure to appropriate elemental or celestial influences, and periodic reconsecration to renew and refocus magical alignment. Tools develop deeper magical connections through consistent use and proper care, often becoming increasingly attuned to their practitioners over years of magical partnership.

LIVING PLANT TALISMANS AND GUARDIANS

Unlike crafted tools created from harvested plant materials, living plant talismans maintain their connection to continuous growth and vital life force. These botanical guardians bring the power of ongoing plant consciousness into magical practice, creating relationships with fully alive allies rather than working solely with plant parts or essences. Incorporating living plants as magical partners adds an incomparable dimension to green witchcraft, connecting practitioners to plant intelligences that actively respond, grow, and evolve alongside them.

Strategic placement maximizes living plant magic throughout home and practice spaces. Entryway plants serve as primary guardians, filtering energies entering your space while establishing initial magical impressions. Traditional threshold plants include rosemary for protection, basil for prosperity welcome, or aloe for gentle healing energy. Window plants intercept and transform incoming light energy while mediating between inner and outer worlds—hanging protective plants like spider plant or English ivy helps transform external energies before they fully enter your space. Altar plants maintain continuous living presence within sacred space, their growth and cycles reflecting ongoing magical development. Bedroom plants influence dream states and rest quality—lavender promotes peaceful sleep, while jasmine enhances prophetic dreaming. This intentional placement creates a comprehensive network of living guardians throughout your environment.

Guide: Rosemary Guardian for Home Protection
Magical Purpose: Establishes a living protective presence that continuously wards the home entrance while providing fresh protective herb for magical use.
Requirements:
• Healthy rosemary plant (preferably already established)
• Container with good drainage if using potted specimen
• Location receiving at least 6 hours of sunlight daily
• Well-draining soil mixture
• Consecrated water for ritual feeding

Selection Guidelines: Choose a rosemary plant that exhibits vitality and strong aroma. If selecting from a nursery, spend time with different specimens and choose the one that feels most responsive to your energy. Upright varieties work well for formal protection, while prostrate varieties excel at creating protective boundaries.
Placement: Position within 3 feet of your main entrance, either flanking the doorway or visible from the threshold. If

climate allows, plant directly in the ground for strongest protection. In harsh climates, use a substantial container that can be moved indoors during extreme weather.

Consecration Ritual:

1 Before placing the rosemary in its permanent position, perform this consecration:

2 Address the plant directly, introducing yourself and your intention: "Guardian of this threshold, I welcome you to your post of protection. I ask that you stand watch over this entrance, permitting positive energies to enter while turning away negativity and harm."

3 Water the plant with moon water or water containing a pinch of protective salt while visualizing protective blue light emanating from its branches.

4 Circle the plant three times clockwise, defining its protective boundary.

5 Place a small protective stone (black tourmaline works well) in the soil at the plant's base to amplify its protective properties.

Maintenance Relationship:

1 Develop regular communication through daily or weekly acknowledgment—a simple greeting and gratitude for its protective service.

2 When watering, add intention to the water by holding it between your palms and visualizing protective energy infusing the liquid.

3 During the waxing moon, speak affirmations of strength and vitality to support the plant's growth.

4 During the waning moon, thank the plant for absorbing and transmuting negative energies.

5 Harvest small amounts for magical use with explicit acknowledgment and gratitude, explaining the purpose of the harvesting.

Seasonal Observances:
• Spring: Offer fresh water and fertilizer while stating intentions for renewed protective strength.
• Summer: At the height of growth, circle the plant with protective intention, reinforcing its guardian role.
• Autumn: Express gratitude for protection provided during active months as the plant's growth slows.
• Winter: If dormancy occurs, assure the plant of your continued relationship despite its resting state.

Harvesting Protocol: When harvesting sprigs for magical use, approach with respect and clear purpose. Explain to the plant exactly how its material will be used and why. Cut cleanly with sharp shears, taking no more than 1/3 of growth at any time. Always leave an offering in exchange—fresh water, organic fertilizer, or a song. This reciprocity maintains positive relationship while ensuring the plant remains healthy enough to fulfill its protective function.

Signs of Magical Activation: A successfully activated rosemary guardian may demonstrate increased aroma when negativity approaches, unusual flowering patterns in response to household events, or growth directed toward areas needing additional protection. Pay attention to these communications and respond appropriately to strengthen your working relationship.

Species selection matches plant properties to specific magical needs. Protective plants with thorns or strong aromatics—roses, rosemary, thorny barberry—excel at boundary enforcement and negative energy repulsion. Prosperity plants with abundant growth habits—jade plants, basil, mint—continuously generate wealth-attracting energy. Healing plants with soothing properties—aloe, lavender, chamomile—create atmospheres conducive to recovery and wellness. Divinatory plants associated with vision and clarity—mugwort, wormwood, bay—enhance psychic awareness and intuitive development. Research traditional magical properties while also developing personal relationships through direct communion with potential plant allies.

Ritual introduction establishes clear magical partnership from the beginning. When bringing a new plant guardian into your space, formally introduce yourself and state the specific role you're requesting the plant to fulfill. Present appropriate offerings based on the plant's needs and the service requested—water, organic fertilizer, or specialized care commitments proportional to the magical function. Create clear energetic boundaries through ritual gestures like circling the plant's container clockwise three times while stating protection parameters, or placing appropriate crystals in the growing medium to amplify specific energetic functions. This formal beginning acknowledges the plant as magical collaborator rather than mere decoration.

Ongoing relationship maintenance strengthens plant talisman effectiveness over time. Regular communication through direct speech, meditation, or energetic exchange builds deeper connection and mutual understanding. Seasonal acknowledgments—special care at solstices and equinoxes, celebration of blooming periods, recognition of dormancy cycles—align your relationship with natural rhythms. Appropriate offerings continue reciprocity, with offerings adjusted to reflect the plant's changing needs and the benefits received from its presence. This continuous relationship development creates increasingly sophisticated magical partnerships as both witch and plant learn each other's patterns and preferences.

Proper handling of plant guardian endings acknowledges the inevitability of transitions within living relationships. When plants complete their natural lifecycle, perform appropriate release rituals expressing gratitude for service rendered. Return plant bodies to earth with respect, perhaps saving seeds for continuation of the particular plant lineage. If separation becomes necessary before natural ending—due to moves, changing magical needs, or unsuitable growing conditions—perform transition rituals finding appropriate new locations or caretakers rather than abandoning magical allies. These conscious completions maintain ethical relationship with plant consciousness while properly closing specific magical agreements.

Through creation and maintenance of these varied herbal tools—portable charms, wooden implements, and living guardians—the green witch establishes a comprehensive network of botanical allies. These tools extend magical intention beyond momentary ritual into continuous presence, creating magical environments that actively support specific purposes and intentions. As these relationships deepen through consistent interaction and proper care, the boundaries between tool and ally blur, transforming herbal magic from the use of plants into collaborative partnership with the green world.

CHAPTER 8

KITCHEN WITCHCRAFT WITH HERBS

The kitchen has long served as the heart of magical practice for countless practitioners throughout history. In this domestic sacred space, the boundaries between nourishment and magic dissolve, creating opportunities for integrated practice that weaves magical intention seamlessly into daily life. Kitchen witchcraft honors the profound magical potential in everyday cooking and food preparation, transforming routine meals into intentional magical acts. This chapter explores three essential aspects of herbal kitchen magic: cooking and baking with magical herbs, brewing magical teas and potions, and creating preserved herbal preparations that extend seasonal magic throughout the year.

MAGICAL COOKING AND BAKING WITH HERBS

The preparation of food with magical intention represents one of humanity's oldest and most consistent magical practices. Long before the formal separation of medicine, magic, and culinary arts, our ancestors understood food as a vehicle for both physical nourishment and magical transformation. Contemporary kitchen witches reclaim this integrated understanding, recognizing that herbs added to everyday cooking carry their magical properties into the body and spirit of those who consume them. This conscious cooking transforms ordinary meals into magical operations that support specific intentions while providing essential physical sustenance.

The magical kitchen operates through principles of correspondence and intention similar to other magical workings, but with the significant addition of physical ingestion. When magical herbs are consumed, their properties enter the body directly, creating effects that operate simultaneously on physical, energetic, and spiritual levels. This direct incorporation allows for particularly potent and holistic magical influence. However, this potency necessitates careful attention to both magical properties and physical safety. Kitchen witchcraft requires thorough knowledge of herb edibility, appropriate dosages, potential contraindications, and food safety practices alongside magical correspondences.

Intention setting forms the foundation of effective kitchen magic. Before beginning food preparation, clarify exactly what magical influence you wish to incorporate into the meal. Connect this intention to the occasion, the needs of those who will partake, and the seasonal or cyclical context of the gathering. This clear purpose guides subsequent herb selection and preparation methods. While cooking, maintain conscious focus on your intention through visualization, spoken affirmations, or songs and chants traditional to kitchen magic. This sustained attention transforms mechanical food preparation into deliberate magical action.

Herb selection balances magical properties with culinary appropriateness. Rosemary brings protection and mental clarity while complementing many savory dishes with its pine-like aroma. Basil attracts prosperity and harmony while adding fresh, slightly sweet notes to foods. Cinnamon accelerates magical effects and attracts abundance while warming both sweet and savory recipes. Thyme brings courage and strength while offering versatile savory applications. Garlic provides powerful protection while serving as a culinary foundation across countless traditions. This harmony between magical and culinary properties allows kitchen witches to create foods that satisfy on multiple levels simultaneously.

Recipe: Prosperity Herb Bread
Magical Purpose: Creates a simple bread that attracts abundance, opportunity, and wealth while providing nourishing sustenance.
Ingredients:
- 3 cups all-purpose or bread flour
- 1 tablespoon active dry yeast
- 1 teaspoon salt
- 1 tablespoon honey or sugar

- 2 tablespoons olive oil
- 1 cup warm water (approximately)
- 2 tablespoons fresh basil, finely chopped (prosperity, harmony)
- 1 tablespoon fresh rosemary, chopped (protection, ensuring prosperity comes without harm)
- 1 teaspoon dried thyme (courage to pursue opportunities)
- ½ teaspoon ground cinnamon (accelerates wealth attraction)
- A few saffron threads if available (solar energy, happiness in abundance)

Magical Timing: Prepare during the waxing moon, ideally on Thursday (Jupiter's day) or Sunday (Sun's day) for enhanced prosperity energy. The hour of Jupiter or Venus enhances abundance aspects.

Preparation with Intention:

1 Begin by cleansing your kitchen space—wipe counters with prosperity-drawing vinegar (apple cider vinegar with a few coins soaked in it) or burning prosperity incense briefly.

2 Set up a small prosperity altar in your kitchen workspace with symbols of abundance meaningful to you—coins, green candles, or prosperity symbols.

3 Combine yeast with warm water and honey, speaking: "As these elements activate and grow, so too does abundance flow into my life."

4 While the yeast activates, mix dry ingredients in a large bowl, adding each herb with intention:

◦ As you add basil: "Basil of abundance, draw prosperity to this bread and to all who eat it."

- As you add rosemary: "Rosemary of protection, ensure this prosperity comes without harm or loss."
- As you add thyme: "Thyme of courage, grant strength to recognize and seize opportunity."
- As you add cinnamon: "Cinnamon of acceleration, quicken the flow of abundance into our lives."
- If using saffron: "Saffron of the sun, bring joy and happiness with this prosperity."

5 When combining wet and dry ingredients, visualize golden light infusing the mixture, representing prosperity entering your life.

6 While kneading the dough, chant softly: "With these hands, abundance grows; with this bread, prosperity flows."

7 Allow bread to rise in a warm place, seeing how its expansion represents growing abundance in your life.

8 Before placing in the oven, carve a prosperity symbol (dollar sign, pentacle, or personal abundance sigil) into the top of the loaf.

9 Bake until golden and aromatic, seeing the transformation by fire as the activation of your prosperity magic.

Serving and Activation: Share this bread with your household or prosperity partners, explaining its intention if appropriate. As you eat, visualize the herbal properties spreading throughout your body, activating prosperity consciousness and attracting abundance opportunities. Save the end piece of the loaf on your prosperity altar until the next prosperity work to maintain continuity of intention.

Safety Note: Ensure all herbs used are culinary varieties and properly identified. Decorative or ornamental herbs from florists or garden centers may be treated with chemicals unsafe for consumption.

Timing considerations enhance kitchen magic effectiveness. Align cooking with natural cycles—waxing moon periods for magic focused on increase and attraction, waning moon for reduction and banishing. Planetary days and hours provide additional magical alignment—Thursday cooking for prosperity and expansion, Friday for love and harmony, Sunday for vitality and success. Seasonal cooking with locally available herbs connects kitchen magic to immediate environmental energies, strengthening connections to local land spirits while accessing peak herbal potency. These timing considerations transform routine meal scheduling into conscious participation in natural cycles.

Traditional recipes passed through generations often contain implicit magical knowledge embedded within culinary instruction. Many cultural food traditions incorporate herbs specifically for their magical and medicinal properties alongside their flavor contributions. Italian cuisine's abundant use of protective basil, rosemary, and garlic reflects traditional concern with warding off negative influences and illness. Middle Eastern use of mint supports digestive health while bringing prosperity. Mexican incorporation of cleansing oregano and protective chili maintains both physical and energetic wellbeing. Reconnecting with cultural food traditions—either from your own heritage or respectfully learned from other traditions—provides access to generations of kitchen magic wisdom refined through practical application.

Contemporary adaptations allow kitchen witches to accommodate modern dietary needs while maintaining magical effectiveness. Herbalism flexibly addresses dietary restrictions through thoughtful substitutions—celiac practitioners can incorporate magical herbs into gluten-free baking, vegan witches can infuse plant-based proteins with strengthening herbs, and those with specific allergies can identify safe magical alternatives that carry similar properties. These adaptations require creativity and experimentation but often result in highly personalized magical cooking practices precisely tailored to individual needs and circumstances. This adaptability demonstrates one of kitchen witchcraft's greatest strengths—its ability to evolve while maintaining core magical principles.

BREWING MAGICAL TEAS AND POTIONS

The brewing of herbal infusions represents perhaps the most accessible form of kitchen magic, requiring minimal equipment while providing immediate and potent magical effects. The simple act of extracting herbal properties into water creates magical tools that simultaneously affect physical, emotional, and spiritual levels through direct consumption. From morning tea rituals to elaborate ceremonial brews, magical infusions offer flexible applications adaptable to nearly any magical purpose or lifestyle circumstance.

Water itself brings significant magical properties to tea and potion preparation. Its receptive nature readily accepts and conducts herbal energies, while its essential role in biological functions allows it to carry magic throughout the entire system. Water's associations with emotion and the unconscious make water-based preparations particularly effective for emotional healing, intuitive development, and dreamwork. The temperature of water used influences the extraction process both physically and magically—hot water extractions bring active, expansive energy while cold infusions carry receptive, introspective properties. These foundational water qualities establish the magical base upon which specific herbal properties build.

Intention setting holds particular importance in beverage magic due to the intimate nature of consumption. Before beginning preparation, clearly establish your specific magical purpose—general wellness, specific healing, emotional balance, spiritual opening, or other defined intention. Communicate this intention directly to the herbs as you measure them, acknowledging their assistance in your magical work. Maintain focused attention throughout preparation, infusing each step with conscious purpose through visualization, spoken charms, or appropriate symbols drawn in the water's surface. This clear intention transforms simple herb-water combinations into potent magical tools directed toward specific purposes.

Single-herb infusions allow direct access to specific magical properties with clarity and precision. Chamomile tea brings calming, stress-reducing properties beneficial before divinatory work requiring emotional equilibrium. Rosemary infusion enhances memory and mental clarity while providing protective properties. Lemon balm tea uplifts mood and attracts positive emotional experiences. Peppermint energizes and stimulates while clearing away obstacles and stagnation. These focused, single-herb preparations provide straightforward magical tools for specific purposes, ideal for both beginning practitioners and those requiring precise magical influences.

Recipe: Dream Enhancement Tea

Magical Purpose: Enhances dream recall, promotes prophetic dreaming, and facilitates conscious dreamwork while providing gentle relaxation for sound sleep.

Ingredients:

- 1 teaspoon dried mugwort (dream enhancement, psychic opening) *Use with caution during pregnancy*
- 1 teaspoon dried chamomile flowers (relaxation, gentle sleep)
- ½ teaspoon dried lavender buds (peaceful sleep, spiritual awareness)
- ½ teaspoon dried rose petals (emotional healing in dreams)
- Small pinch of cinnamon (activation, enchantment)
- 8 ounces fresh spring water or filtered water
- Optional: 1 teaspoon honey (preferably raw) or lemon for taste and added magical properties

Magical Timing: Prepare during the hour after sunset as day transitions to night, ideally during the waxing to full moon when intuitive powers are heightened. Monday (Moon day) enhances dream properties.

Equipment:

- Ceramic or glass teapot (avoid metal for dream herbs)
- Moonstone or amethyst crystal (optional)

- White or purple candle
- Strainer
- Dedicated dream tea cup (preferably white, blue, or purple)

Preparation Ritual:

1 Begin by cleansing your preparation space with appropriate incense (lavender or jasmine works well).

2 Light a white or purple candle, stating: "I light this flame to illuminate the pathways between worlds."

3 If using crystal, place it beside your teapot, saying: "Crystal of vision, enhance the dream potential of this brew."

4 Heat water until just before boiling (too hot water will create bitterness and damage delicate magical properties).

5 Place herbs in teapot, holding each briefly before adding:

- As you add mugwort: "Mugwort of vision, open the gates of dreaming."
- As you add chamomile: "Chamomile of peace, grant restful sleep that dreams may flourish."
- As you add lavender: "Lavender of tranquility, create safe space for dream journeys."
- As you add rose: "Rose of the heart, bring healing visions and emotional clarity."
- As you add cinnamon: "Cinnamon of power, activate these herbs in harmony."

6 Pour water over herbs in a clockwise circular motion, saying: "Waters of intuition, extract the wisdom of these plants."

7 Cover immediately to retain essential oils and magical properties.

8 Place hands around the teapot, visualizing soft silver-blue light entering the brew.

9 Allow to steep for 7-10 minutes while focusing on your specific dream intention.

10 Strain into your dedicated dream cup, adding honey if desired with the affirmation: "Sweetness in dreams, clarity in visions."

Usage Instructions: Drink this tea 30-60 minutes before bedtime in a quiet setting. While drinking, visualize yourself remembering your dreams clearly upon waking. Keep a dream journal and pen beside your bed to record impressions immediately upon awakening. This tea may be consumed up to three times weekly—more frequent use can create dependency or tolerance to its magical effects.

Cautions: Mugwort may cause vivid or intense dreams and should be reduced or eliminated if dreams become disturbing. Pregnant individuals should avoid mugwort entirely. Those on sedative medications should consult healthcare providers before using relaxing herbs like chamomile and lavender.

Complex herbal formulations combine multiple herbs into synergistic preparations with sophisticated magical effects. Effective formulations balance primary herbs addressing the central magical purpose with supporting herbs that enhance or direct the primary effects. Balancing herbs moderate intensity and provide centering, while catalyst herbs activate the blend and accelerate effects. Traditional formulation follows the rule of three, five, or seven herbs—odd numbers traditionally associated with magical potency. This mathematical structure guides beginning formulators while providing magical resonance through numerical correspondence. As experience develops, practitioners often move beyond strict numerical formulas into intuitive blending guided by direct herbal relationships.

Ceremonial consumption transforms ordinary drinking into ritual magic through conscious engagement with the preparation. Create appropriate space through cleansing, boundary setting, and establishing sacred intent. Incorporate meaningful gestures—stirring clockwise to build energy or counterclockwise to diminish, passing cups through incense smoke for purification, or speaking blessings over prepared brews. Mindful sipping with attention to taste, temperature, and bodily effects grounds magical awareness in sensory experience. These ceremonial elements elevate simple consumption into conscious magical practice, enhancing effectiveness through focused engagement.

Safety considerations hold paramount importance in consumable magic. Verify herb identity with absolute certainty, using reliable field guides and reputable suppliers. Research contraindications, medication interactions, and safety during pregnancy or breastfeeding before incorporating herbs into consumable preparations. Start with small amounts of unfamiliar herbs to identify possible sensitivities or allergic reactions. Maintain appropriate dosage awareness, recognizing that magical effectiveness does not necessarily increase with quantity—often quite the opposite, with moderate amounts providing optimal magical effects while minimizing potential physical concerns. These safety practices ensure that magical brewing remains beneficial on all levels.

HERBAL HONEYS, VINEGARS, AND PRESERVES

The magical preservation of herbs through honey, vinegar, alcohol, and sugar extends seasonal plant energy throughout the year while creating stable, versatile magical tools. These traditional preservation methods each contribute distinct magical properties to herbal preparations while extracting and maintaining plant constituents. Understanding these preservation techniques allows witches to capture peak seasonal herb energy for ongoing magical use while participating in ancient traditions of magical food preservation.

Honey preservations carry inherent properties of sweetening, attraction, and binding. The natural antimicrobial properties of honey preserve herbal constituents while its symbolic golden abundance connects to prosperity and solar energy. Rose petal honey attracts love and softens emotional wounds through its combination of floral heart magic and honey's sweetness. Thyme honey builds courage and strength while providing natural immune support. Lavender honey brings peaceful sleep and stress reduction. These preparations function simultaneously as magical tools, culinary ingredients, and healing remedies—exemplifying kitchen witchcraft's integration of multiple purposes into single preparations.

Technique: Creating Magical Infused Honey
Magical Purpose: Captures and preserves specific herbal

magical properties in honey for extended use in magical cooking, ritual work, and healing applications.

Base Materials:
- 1 cup raw, unfiltered honey (local if possible)
- Clean glass jar with tight-fitting lid
- 1/4 to 1/3 cup dried herbs or 1/2 cup fresh herbs
- Wooden or bamboo stirring wand (never metal)
- Cheesecloth or fine strainer
- Labels and marking pen
- Optional: crystal corresponding to magical purpose

Preparation Variations by Magical Intent:
For Love and Heart Healing:
- 1/4 cup dried rose petals
- 1 tablespoon dried hibiscus flowers
- 1 teaspoon dried lavender
- 2-3 small pieces of rose quartz
- *Best prepared on Friday during Venus hours with pink or red candle burning*

For Protection and Purification:
- 3 tablespoons dried rosemary
- 1 tablespoon dried thyme
- 1 teaspoon dried sage
- Small piece of black tourmaline
- *Best prepared on Tuesday during Mars hours with purple or black candle burning*

For Prosperity and Abundance:
- 3 tablespoons dried mint
- 1 teaspoon cinnamon chips
- 1 teaspoon dried basil
- Small citrine crystal
- *Best prepared on Thursday during Jupiter hours with green or gold candle burning*

Basic Preparation Method:
1 Begin by cleansing your workspace and tools with appropriate incense or herbal smoke.
2 Warm honey gently in a double boiler until it flows easily, but never heat above 110°F (43°C) to preserve raw properties.
3 Place chosen dried herbs in your jar, holding each herb briefly while affirming its magical purpose.
4 If using a crystal, cleanse it thoroughly and place it in the bottom of the jar as a magical anchor.
5 Pour warm honey over the herbs slowly, leaving about 1/2 inch of space at the top.
6 Use your wooden wand to stir clockwise, speaking your intention clearly: "By herb and honey sweet, bring [specific intention] complete."
7 Cap tightly and place in a warm window where the honey will receive several hours of sunlight daily.
8 Turn the jar three times clockwise each day, restating your intention.
9 Allow to infuse for:
  - 2 weeks for dried herbs
  - 4-6 weeks for fresh herbs

- Lunar cycle (new moon to new moon) for workings tied to lunar energy

10 When infusion is complete, strain through cheesecloth for clear honey, or leave herbs in for stronger magical properties and visual appeal.

11 Label with herbs used, date prepared, magical intention, and best-use-by date (generally one year).

Usage Applications:
- Add to ritual cakes or cookies for celebration magic
- Use to sweeten magical teas aligned with your intention
- Drizzle over ritual bread or fruits during sabbat celebrations
- Apply to magical seals on letters or petition papers
- Use small amounts to anoint candles for corresponding magical purposes
- Include in healing remedies that align with magical purpose

Storage Notes: Keep in a cool, dark place. Honey rarely spoils, but herbal inclusions may change over time. If honey crystallizes, warm gently in a water bath to restore flowing consistency. Magical potency may diminish after one year, though physical preservation remains longer.

Vinegar infusions embody transformative, cleansing, and preservative magic. The acidic nature of vinegar extracts different plant constituents than other menstruums, particularly drawing mineral components with grounding properties. Rosemary vinegar creates powerful cleansing washes for homes and magical tools. Sage vinegar disperses negative energy while preserving the herb's cleansing properties. Four Thieves vinegar blends—traditional protective formulas combining multiple antimicrobial herbs—provide powerful protective magic against both physical and energetic contagion. These preparations bridge magical, medicinal, and culinary applications through their versatile properties and applications.

Preserved fruits and herbal syrups capture peak seasonal energy in forms that maintain magical properties while providing delightful culinary applications. Blackberry preserves hold protective and healing properties while connecting to late summer abundance. Elder syrups maintain immune-supporting properties alongside the elder tree's protective and transitional magic. Rose syrups capture heart-opening, love-attracting properties in forms that can be added to beverages, desserts, or ritual foods year-round. These sweet preparations serve multiple magical functions while providing pleasurable consumption experiences—magical tools that delight the senses while directing specific energies.

Timing significantly impacts preserved preparations. Harvesting at points of peak plant energy—flowers at full bloom, berries at perfect ripeness, herbs just before flowering—provides optimal starting materials with maximum magical potency. Moon phase alignment enhances specific magical properties—waxing moon for preparations intended to attract or increase, full moon for maximum power and manifestation, waning moon for banishing or diminishing unwanted conditions. Seasonal alignment connects preserves to the wheel of the year—spring preparations capture initiatory energy, midsummer preserves embody peak manifestation, autumn preparations center on harvest and abundance, winter preparations focus on rest and inner work. These timing considerations transform simple food preservation into conscious participation in natural cycles.

Kitchen witchcraft integrates magic into daily life through the fundamental acts of nourishing self and community. By approaching cooking, brewing, and preserving as magical acts, practitioners dissolve artificial boundaries between mundane and magical while creating consistent, practical magical practice integrated into necessary daily activities. This seamless incorporation of magic into everyday life represents one of kitchen witchcraft's greatest strengths—the ability to maintain continuous magical practice without requiring separate time or elaborate ritual structures. Through these accessible, practical techniques, the kitchen witch creates ongoing magical influence through the essential acts of preparing and sharing food and drink.

CHAPTER 9

HERBAL MAGIC THROUGHOUT THE SEASONS

The cycle of seasons provides a natural framework for magical herbalism, offering changing energies, plants, and opportunities throughout the year. By aligning magical practice with these seasonal shifts, the green witch accesses the powerful currents of natural energy that flow through each phase of the annual cycle. This chapter explores the distinct herbal magic of spring, summer, and autumn, examining how each season offers unique botanical allies and magical possibilities. Through conscious engagement with these seasonal energies, practitioners develop magical work that resonates harmoniously with the world around them while accessing the peak potency of herbs at their appointed times.

SPRING HERBS AND RENEWAL RITUALS

Spring embodies the magical energies of awakening, renewal, and initiation. As the earth reawakens from winter dormancy, a powerful surge of life force rises through plants, creating a natural current of energy that supports magical work focused on new beginnings, growth, and transformation. This seasonal energy offers particularly potent support for spells involving fresh starts, personal renewal, creative inspiration, and the initial stages of manifestation. By working with spring's distinctive botanical allies and magical currents, the witch harnesses natural momentum to propel new magical workings into successful manifestation.

Spring's earliest herbs, often called "spring ephemerals," carry unique magical properties connected to their remarkable ability to emerge through the last remnants of winter. These plants—including snowdrops, crocuses, and early violets—appear while much of the landscape remains dormant, embodying breakthrough energy and the ability to overcome obstacles. Their magical correspondences center on breaking through barriers, dispelling stagnation, and initiating movement after periods of restriction. Working with these early bloomers supports magical efforts to overcome inertia, begin difficult projects, or emerge from challenging personal circumstances with renewed purpose and direction.

Dandelion (Taraxacum officinale) represents one of spring's most powerful magical herbs, though often overlooked due to its commonplace status. This persistent plant brings remarkably multifaceted magical properties: its ability to break through seemingly impenetrable surfaces symbolizes overcoming obstacles; its transformation from golden flower to ethereal seedhead represents complete magical cycles; its deep taproot connects to hidden knowledge and resources; its bitter properties clear stagnation on all levels. Spring dandelion magic particularly supports communication, divination, and wish fulfillment. Collect young leaves before flowering for purification rituals and fresh starts. Harvest flowers at noon on clear days for solar magic and wish-making. Use root collected during spring growth for connecting with hidden knowledge and tapping inner resources. These seasonal applications access dandelion's specific spring energy while honoring its remarkable magical versatility.

Spring Ritual: Dandelion Renewal Bath
Magical Purpose: Creates a powerful cleansing experience that releases winter's stagnation, activates personal energy, and aligns with spring's growth potential.
Ingredients:
- 1 cup fresh young dandelion leaves and flowers
- 1/2 cup fresh violet flowers and leaves (purification, protection)
- 1/4 cup fresh chickweed (releases what no longer serves)
- 3 sprigs fresh mint (energizing, awakening)
- 1 tablespoon sea salt (grounding, cleansing)
- 1 quartz crystal (amplification)
- 1 green candle
- Muslin bag or cheesecloth for herbs

Timing: Perform during the waxing moon in early spring

when dandelions first bloom abundantly, ideally at dawn or sunset to align with transitional energies.

Preparation:

1 Harvest herbs with gratitude early in the morning after dew has dried but before full sun.

2 Create a sacred space in your bathroom through cleansing and boundary setting.

3 Fill the bathtub with comfortably warm water, not hot (excessive heat damages volatile herb properties).

4 Place all herbs in muslin bag and hold between your hands, stating: "Winter's hold now fades away, Spring's renewal begins today. With these herbs of early green, I cleanse my energy completely clean."

5 Submerge the herb bag in water and allow to steep while the tub fills completely.

6 Add sea salt in a clockwise spiral pattern, saying: "Salt of earth, ground and clear all that no longer serves me here."

7 Light the green candle and place safely near the bath, stating: "Fire of transformation, witness this renewal."

8 Place crystal in water (ensure it's water-safe) to amplify the herbal properties.

Bathing Ritual:

1 Enter the bath mindfully, visualizing yourself crossing a threshold into spring energy.

2 Use the herb bag as a gentle scrub, moving from feet upward toward the heart, then from hands inward, and finally around the face and head.

3 While scrubbing, name specifically what you are releasing:

"I release stagnation... I release doubt... I release winter's heaviness..."

4 Immerse fully if comfortable, visualizing the herb-infused water dissolving any remaining energetic residue from winter.

5 When ready to complete, state clearly: "Cleansed and renewed, I align with spring's potential. I welcome growth, new beginnings, and fresh energy into my life."

6 Exit the bath and allow yourself to air dry if possible, or blot gently with a white towel.

Completion: Pour a small amount of the bath water onto earth as an offering, thanking the plant allies for their assistance. The remaining bath water can be released normally. Use the damp herbs as compost or return to the earth in a natural area.

Follow-up Practice: For the next three days, begin each morning by placing your hands over your heart and repeating: "Spring's renewal flows through me. I am open to new growth and possibilities."

Chickweed (Stellaria media) provides essential spring magic for releasing what no longer serves while creating space for new growth. This ubiquitous early green brings subtle but powerful properties of gentle dissolution, particularly effective for magical work involving the release of habits, relationships, or situations that have overstayed their usefulness. Unlike more dramatic banishing herbs, chickweed works gradually and gently, creating space for new growth without traumatic disruption. Use fresh chickweed in baths for releasing stagnant energy accumulated during winter. Add to spring cleaning floor washes to dissolve lingering negative influences from living spaces. Incorporate into sachets designed to gently release emotional attachments that prevent forward movement. These applications harness chickweed's natural correspondence with spring's transitional energy between release and initiation.

Violet (Viola spp.) carries the magical properties of spiritual protection, modesty strength, and faithfulness. These early-blooming flowers combine apparent delicacy with remarkable resilience, making them particularly suited for magic involving hidden strength, protection of vulnerable new beginnings, and subtle influence rather than overt power. Spring violets support magical works for enhancing intuition, protecting new creative projects, and establishing faithful connections. Collect flowers with morning dew still present for heightened magical potency in matters of psychic development. Add leaves to baths for purification with protective qualities. Create violet water for cleansing ritual tools dedicated to divinatory purposes. These spring applications capture violet's ephemeral energy at its peak while honoring the plant's traditional associations with hidden power and faithful protection.

Cleansing rituals represent essential spring magical work, clearing accumulated energetic stagnation from winter while creating space for new magical possibilities. Comprehensive spring cleaning becomes magical practice when approached with intention and incorporating appropriate herbal allies—lemon-infused water with a few drops of pine essential oil cleanses surfaces while dispersing stagnant energy; floor-washes incorporating chickweed, violet, and broom flowers remove lingering winter heaviness; smudging with spring herbs like cedar tips and pine needles purifies air and aura simultaneously. These cleansing practices honor the natural energy of the season while preparing space for the year's magical work ahead.

Personal renewal magic aligns perfectly with spring's natural energy. Ritual baths incorporating early spring herbs facilitate energetic revival and realignment with seasonal flow. Wardrobe cleansing with herbal sachets placed among clean clothes infuses daily life with intentional seasonal energy. Seed-planting rituals where magical intentions are literally planted with appropriate botanical allies create powerful sympathetic magic—plant sweet basil seeds with prosperity intentions, rosemary with protective purposes, borage with courage goals. These personal renewal practices create magical harmony between practitioner and seasonal energy, establishing foundation for effective magic throughout the coming growth cycle.

SUMMER ABUNDANCE AND SOLAR HERBS

Midsummer marks the peak of solar energy and botanical abundance, creating a magical environment charged with manifestation power, culmination, and exuberant expression. The summer solstice—the longest day and shortest night—represents maximum light and external activity, supporting magic focused on full manifestation, protection, strength, and passion. Following this peak, high summer brings lush growth and abundant flowering, sustaining powerful currents of manifestation energy before the eventual turn toward harvest. This potent seasonal phase provides exceptional support for magical work involving achievement, recognition, and bringing projects to successful completion.

Sun-infused preparations capture solar energy at its annual height, creating magical tools with concentrated light properties. Solar-infused oils made during the solstice or during the astrological sign of Leo carry particularly potent solar magic suitable for anointing ritual tools, dressing candles, or personal empowerment work. Sun-charged water left in sealed glass containers during peak daylight hours absorbs vital solar energy useful for brewing magical teas, feeding magical plants, or ritual cleansing. Sun teas brewed in direct sunlight combine herbal properties with solar infusion for double-potency magical beverages. These solar preparations literally capture the light at its yearly maximum, creating magical resources that extend summer's energy into other seasonal phases.

St. John's Wort (Hypericum perforatum) embodies solar magic through multiple signatures—golden flowers resembling miniature suns, red oil that bleeds from crushed buds like captured sunlight, and traditional harvesting at midsummer when solar power peaks. This herb brings protective power specifically against depression, spiritual darkness, and negative energetic influences. Summer St. John's Wort magic specializes in illuminating hidden negativity, dispelling shadows from homes and psyches, and creating boundaries against psychic attack. Harvest flowering tops at noon on or near the summer solstice for maximum solar properties.

Create red St. John's oil through solar infusion for anointing protective amulets and home thresholds. Use in protective sachets placed in vehicles for travel safety during summer journeys. These applications honor the herb's traditional associations with solstice celebration and protective magic against both physical and spiritual threats.

Solar Infusion: St. John's Wort Protective Oil
Magical Purpose: Creates a powerful protective oil that captures peak solar energy along with St. John's Wort's natural defensive properties, useful for anointing people, spaces, and objects against negative influences.
Ingredients:
• Fresh St. John's Wort flowering tops with buds and newly opened flowers
• High-quality olive oil (traditional) or sweet almond oil (for skin applications)
• Clear glass jar with tight-fitting lid
• Red cloth (traditional) or gold cloth
• String or rubber band
• Label and permanent marker
• Small piece of citrine or sunstone (optional)
Timing: For maximum potency, harvest St. John's Wort and begin infusion as close to the summer solstice as possible, when the herb's protective properties peak alongside solar energy. The traditional time is June 24th (St. John's Day), but anytime within the week surrounding the solstice is appropriate. Begin infusion at noon when the sun reaches its daily zenith.

Harvesting Guidelines:
1 Harvest on a clear, sunny day after morning dew has dried but before mid-day heat.
2 Select flowering tops where some buds are still closed and others have just opened.
3 Test readiness by crushing a bud between fingers—it should produce a reddish-purple stain, indicating the presence of hypericin (the active protective constituent).
4 Harvest with gratitude, leaving at least 2/3 of the plant untouched to ensure sustainability.

Preparation:
1 Gently wilt harvested plant material for 2-4 hours to reduce moisture content, spreading on a clean cloth in a warm, shaded spot.
2 Prepare your jar by cleansing with protective incense smoke or moon water.
3 If using a crystal, place it at the bottom of the jar as an energetic anchor.
4 Fill the jar approximately 2/3 full with plant material, pressing gently but not compacting.
5 Pour oil over the plant material until completely covered with an additional inch of oil above.
6 Use a wooden chopstick or wand to release any air bubbles, stirring clockwise and stating your protective intention.
7 Seal the jar tightly and label with date, ingredients, and purpose.
8 Wrap the jar in red or gold cloth, securing with string or rubber band but leaving the top exposed to sunlight.

Solar Infusion Process:

1 Place the wrapped jar in a location that receives direct sunlight for at least 6 hours daily.
2 Each day at noon for the first three days, unwrap, open briefly to release any built-up gases, reseal, and return to sunlight.
3 Continue solar infusion for 3-6 weeks, turning the jar a quarter turn clockwise each day while stating: "By sun above and fire within, Protection grows again and again."
4 The oil will gradually develop a deep red color, indicating successful extraction of protective compounds.
5 When the oil reaches a rich ruby color, strain through cheesecloth into a clean dark glass bottle.

Magical Uses:
• Anoint doorways and windows to prevent negative energies from entering
• Apply to protective amulets to charge and activate them
• Draw protective symbols on candles before burning for safeguarding rituals
• Place a few drops on the corners of your bed for protection during sleep
• Add to baths for cleansing negative attachments and spiritual protection

Storage and Potency: Store in a cool, dark place for maximum shelf life. The protective properties remain potent for approximately one year. The deep red color is an indicator of magical potency—when the color begins to fade significantly, it's time to create a fresh batch.

Caution: St. John's Wort oil can cause photosensitivity when applied to skin exposed to direct sunlight. For topical applications, dilute appropriately and avoid sun exposure to treated areas.

Lavender (Lavandula spp.) reaches peak magical potency during summer flowering, offering powerful properties for peace, purification, and healing during this active season. While available year-round in dried form, summer lavender offers exceptional magical potency through its concentrated essential oils and vital flowering energy. Summer lavender magic excels in creating calm within activity—maintaining emotional balance during busy periods, establishing peaceful sanctuaries amid high summer's intense energy, and supporting restful sleep despite extended daylight. Harvest flower spikes when approximately half the individual buds have opened for optimal essential oil content and magical potency. Create dream pillows for peaceful summer sleep during warm nights. Prepare lavender wands by weaving fresh stems with ribbon for year-round access to summer's peace. These applications capture lavender's distinctive summer energy while providing magical tools that extend its benefits beyond the growing season.

Mugwort (Artemisia vulgaris) develops its strongest magical properties during summer months when its silvery foliage and distinctive aroma reach peak development. This herb's primary magical associations involve psychic development, dreamwork, and divination—perfectly complementing summer's thinned veil between worlds and enhanced intuitive potential during this active phase. Summer mugwort magic supports dream journeying, enhances intuitive practices, and strengthens divinatory workings. Harvest leafy stems before flowering for dream enhancement preparations. Create protective wreaths incorporating mugwort with flowering St. John's Wort for entryway protection. Prepare divination incense combining mugwort with summer roses and lavender for scrying during summer's waning days. These magical applications access mugwort's peak properties while honoring its traditional associations with psychic opening and spiritual protection.

Summer solstice celebrations create magical focal points that capture and direct peak solar energy. Fire-centered rituals honor the sun at its zenith while acknowledging the coming decline, creating magical containers for transformation work. Solar water infusions prepared during solstice sunrise carry concentrated light energy for year-round use in rituals requiring illumination, revelation, or truth-seeking. Flower mandalas created from summer's abundant blossoms offer magical tools for manifestation, with precise petal arrangements directing focused intention into physical form. These solstice practices acknowledge seasonal transition points where magical energy concentrates and becomes particularly accessible for intentional direction.

Sun preservation techniques extend summer's magical energy beyond its natural season. Carefully dried summer herbs and flowers retain significant solar properties when harvested at appropriate times and dried using proper methods that maintain essential oils and color. Infused honey captures both the sweetness and light of summer in preserved form, with each flower variety contributing its specific magical properties alongside summer sunshine energy. Sun-charged crystals cleansed and programmed during peak daylight hours retain solar programming for magical work throughout darker seasons. These preservation practices acknowledge the wheel of the year while creating magical continuity between seasonal high points and transitions.

AUTUMN HARVESTS AND TRANSFORMATIVE PLANT MAGIC

Autumn combines abundant harvest energy with the beginning of the inward turn toward winter dormancy. This transitional season offers powerful magical currents supporting completion, preservation, and preparation for inner work. The autumn equinox marks the balance point where light and darkness achieve temporary equilibrium before darkness begins its increase, creating a magical environment particularly conducive to balance work, justice magic, and harvest completion. Following this pivotal point, late autumn brings deepening introspection alongside final harvests, supporting transformative magic that bridges external achievement and internal processing. This complex seasonal phase provides exceptional support for magical work involving completion, preservation, transformation, and preparation for spiritual hibernation.

Seed-saving practices represent essential autumn magic, preserving life potential through the coming dormancy while selecting for desired magical and physical traits. Carefully collected seeds from magical garden plants carry concentrated life potential alongside specific magical properties—calendula seeds preserve healing energy in dormant form, sunflower seeds capture summer's solar power in compact packages, moonflower seeds contain night mysteries and dream potential. Proper magical seed saving involves both physical technique—ensuring appropriate maturity, drying methods, and storage conditions—and magical consciousness—collecting during appropriate moon phases, blessing with specific intentions for future growth, and storing with appropriate talisman correspondences. These combined practices create magical continuity between growing seasons while establishing relationships with plant allies across generations.

Root harvesting forms a central autumn magical practice, accessing the concentrated underground energy developed throughout the growing season. As plants redirect their energy from aerial growth to root systems in preparation for winter dormancy, root magical properties reach peak potency. Dandelion roots harvested in fall bring significantly stronger grounding and manifestation properties than spring-dug specimens. Echinacea roots collected after several killing frosts develop enhanced protective and strengthening magic alongside their immunological benefits. Valerian roots gathered during the waning moon of late autumn provide powerful dream magic and emotional balancing properties. These autumn root harvests access the plants' most concentrated energy while honoring the natural cycle of growth and dormancy.

Root Harvesting Ritual: Autumn Angelica

Magical Purpose: Harvests angelica root at its peak magical potency for protective magic against negative spiritual influences, enhancing psychic defense, and creating powerful boundaries against harmful energies.

Materials:
- Garden-grown angelica plant, at least two years old
- Digging fork or spade
- Pruning shears
- Clean cloth for wiping soil
- Basket lined with dark cloth
- Sharp knife for processing
- Offering materials (water, corn meal, or tobacco)
- Small bell or singing bowl
- White or purple candle

Timing: Harvest after the first killing frost but before the ground freezes, ideally during the dark moon or waning moon in late autumn when the plant's energy has fully retreated to the roots. Morning hours after dew has dried are traditional for protective herbs.

Preparation: Before harvesting day, spend time with the angelica plant for several days, explaining your intention to harvest and expressing gratitude for its protective service. This preparation creates clear communication and respect rather than sudden taking.

Harvesting Ceremony:

1 Begin by creating sacred space around the angelica plant. Define a circle using sound (bell ringing) or by sprinkling a protective mixture of salt and dried rosemary around your working area.

2 Light a white or purple candle, stating: "I bring light to this work of harvest, with respect for the plant spirit and clear protective intention."

3 Address the angelica directly: "Angelica, guardian and protector, I approach you with respect and gratitude. I seek to harvest your root for continued protection work, Carrying your powers forward through the dormant time. I ask your permission and blessing for this harvest."

4 Pause and listen/feel for a response. If you sense resistance, consider postponing or harvesting only a portion of the plant.

5 Present your offering, placing it near the base of the plant.

6 Using the digging fork, carefully loosen the soil around the root system, working at least 8 inches away from the central stalk to avoid damage.

7 Gradually expose the root system by removing soil with hands, maintaining as much root integrity as possible.

8 Once exposed, use pruning shears to cut the aerial parts about 2 inches above the root crown.

9 Lift the entire root system carefully, expressing gratitude as you raise it from the earth: "From darkness to light, I bring your power forth, With gratitude for your protection and strength. May your magic continue through my respectful work."

10 Place immediately in your prepared basket.

11 Before leaving, fill the hole with some of the original soil mixed with your offering material, thanking the earth for supporting the plant's growth.

Processing for Magical Use:

1 Transport the root to your processing area immediately,

maintaining magical continuity and preventing energetic dissipation.

2 Gently remove excess soil using a soft brush or cloth, preserving as much of the root structure as possible.

3 Divide the root according to your magical needs:

◦ For immediate strong protection work: use a small portion fresh

◦ For ongoing protection through winter: slice sections for drying

◦ For future growth: preserve several small sections with viable buds for replanting

4 For drying portions: cut into 1/4 inch slices for even drying

5 As you cut each piece, state: "Protection divided is protection multiplied, Each piece carries full power of the whole."

6 Dry root slices on screens in a dark, well-ventilated area until completely dry and hard.

Storage and Magical Applications:

• Store dried roots in dark glass jars with protective symbols marked on the lids

• Add a small black tourmaline or obsidian crystal to each storage jar to maintain protective properties

• Use in protective amulets carried for spiritual protection

• Add to protective incense for clearing spaces of negative entities

• Include in threshold sachets to prevent harmful energies from entering homes

• Use in protective baths following spiritual healing work or psychic attack

Gratitude Completion: Within one month of harvest,

return to the harvest site with a small token of gratitude—perhaps a crystal, fresh water, or a song. This completes the harvest exchange and maintains good relationship with both the specific plant spirit and the garden space.

Hawthorn (Crataegus spp.) reaches its magical culmination in autumn when its bright red berries ripen against increasingly bare branches. These berries represent the tree's powerful threshold magic concentrated into portable form, carrying the hawthorn's ancient associations with boundaries between worlds, heart healing, and ancestral communication. Autumn hawthorn magic specializes in preparing for winter's liminal states, supporting communication with ancestors during the thinning veil of late autumn, and protecting the vulnerable heart during seasonal transitions. Harvest berries after the first frost has sweetened them, ideally during the waning moon for boundary magic or during the dark moon for ancestral connection. Create protective cordials combining hawthorn berries with brandy and honey for ritual use during ancestral ceremonies. String dried berries into protective garlands for doorways during late autumn when spiritual boundaries thin. These applications honor hawthorn's traditional role as guardian of thresholds between worlds while accessing its specific autumn properties.

Rose hips develop their fullest magical properties during autumn as the plant redirects energy from flowers to seed-bearing fruits. These bright red fruits carry concentrated rose energy in more grounding, substantial form than summer's delicate flowers, bringing heart magic into physical manifestation and practical application. Autumn rose hip magic supports emotional completion work, heart healing following summer's active relationships, and love magic focused on enduring commitment rather than initial attraction. Harvest hips when bright red but still firm, after the first light frost but before deep freezing. Create heart-healing elixirs by infusing rose hips in honey with a small piece of rose quartz crystal. Craft protection-love amulets combining dried rose hips with hawthorn berries for emotional boundaries that remain loving yet firm. These autumn applications access the concentrated manifestation of rose energy while honoring the plant's complete magical cycle from spring leaves through summer flowers to autumn fruits.

Transformative rituals align perfectly with autumn's natural transitional energy. Releasing ceremonies conducted during falling leaves create powerful sympathetic magic for consciously letting go of completed cycles, outgrown relationships, or fulfilled projects. Preservation rituals where summer's achievements become consolidated into lasting form—magical journals recording season accomplishments, preserved foods infused with specific intentions, or essence bottles capturing particular emotional states—create magical continuity between active and dormant phases. Ancestor communication ceremonies utilizing autumn's naturally thinned boundaries between worlds establish connections that support winter's coming introspection phase. These transformative practices acknowledge seasonal transition while creating intentional containers for conscious participation in natural cycles.

Preparation for winter's magical dormancy represents essential autumn work, establishing foundations for the inward journey ahead. Dream journal preparation combines physical creation of dedicated dream recording books with spiritual preparation through autumn herbs supporting dream recall and interpretation. Magical tool maintenance—cleansing, recharging, and proper storage of implements that may rest during winter months—honors the cyclical nature of practice while ensuring readiness for spring's eventual return. Winter altar arrangement incorporating autumn's final flowers, preserved leaves, and harvested seeds creates transitional sacred space bridging seasons while supporting the shifting focus from external to internal work. These preparatory practices acknowledge the wheel of the year while creating conscious transition between magical phases.

Through conscious engagement with these seasonal herbs and magical currents, the green witch develops practice that remains perpetually aligned with natural cycles. Rather than imposing arbitrary magical schedules or working against environmental energies, this seasonally-aligned approach harnesses the substantial power of natural rhythms. Each herb accessed at its peak potency, each ritual performed during appropriate seasonal energy, and each magical tool created in alignment with natural cycles carries enhanced effectiveness through this harmonious relationship with the turning wheel of the year.

CHAPTER 10

HERBAL RITUALS AND CEREMONIES

Moving beyond individual herbal applications into structured magical frameworks, this chapter explores complete herbal rituals and ceremonies. These formalized magical operations combine multiple techniques into cohesive experiences that address specific needs with comprehensive herbal support. By understanding how to design and execute these multi-layered workings, practitioners develop the ability to create powerful magical containers for transformation, healing, and celebration. This chapter examines three primary categories of herbal ritual: cleansing and purification ceremonies, rites of passage support, and seasonal altar practices that honor the turning wheel of the year.

HERBAL CLEANSING AND PURIFICATION RITUALS

Cleansing rituals represent perhaps the most fundamental and universally necessary magical operations. Before beginning any significant magical work, establishing energetic clarity through purification creates essential foundations for effective practice. Herbal allies provide particularly potent support for these cleansing operations, offering physical vehicles for energetic clearing while contributing their specific magical properties to the purification process. Understanding how to design and perform comprehensive herbal cleansing rituals equips practitioners with vital skills applicable across all areas of magical practice.

Space cleansing forms the foundation of environmental magical hygiene, creating clear, intentional energetic conditions for subsequent magical work. Effective herbal space cleansing combines multiple sensory elements—aromatic smoke or sprays for aerial purification, floor washes for surface cleansing, and sound or movement to dislodge stagnant energy pockets. This multi-level approach addresses subtle energetic residue in all aspects of the environment, creating comprehensive purification that prepares space for specific magical purposes. Regular maintenance cleansings maintain magical hygiene, while targeted purifications address specific contamination or prepare spaces for particular magical operations.

Smoke cleansing using appropriate herbal bundles provides one of the most efficient methods for rapid space purification. While white sage has received considerable attention, numerous other herbs offer powerful cleansing properties with less cultural and ecological concern. Garden sage (Salvia officinalis) brings similar purification properties with more sustainable sourcing. Cedar provides protective purification especially effective against lingering negative entities. Rosemary offers clear-minded purification that simultaneously enhances mental focus. Mugwort purifies while opening psychic awareness, particularly useful before divinatory work. These diverse options allow practitioners to select cleansing herbs aligned with both the specific purification needed and appropriate ecological and cultural considerations.

Ritual: Comprehensive Home Purification

Magical Purpose: Creates thorough energetic cleansing throughout a living space, removing stagnant energy, negative influences, and energetic residue while establishing fresh, intentional energy aligned with the inhabitants' purposes.

Materials Needed:
- Herbal purification bundle (recipe follows)
- Herbal floor wash (recipe follows)
- Purification spray (recipe follows)
- White candle
- Bell, chime, or singing bowl
- Bowl of sea salt
- Fresh flowers or living plant
- White cloth

Herbal Purification Bundle:

- 3-4 sprigs garden sage (cleansing, wisdom)
- 2-3 sprigs rosemary (protection, mental clarity)
- 1-2 sprigs thyme (courage, purification)
- 1 small piece of cedar or juniper (longevity of effect, spiritual cleansing)
- 1 bay leaf (victory over negativity)
- Natural cotton string for binding

Gather herbs when dry and in good condition. Hold the herbs together with stems aligned at the bottom. Beginning at the stem end, wrap cotton string tightly around the bundle, working upward in a spiral pattern. Secure with a knot, leaving several inches of string as a handle. Allow to dry completely for 1-2 weeks before using.

Purification Floor Wash:
- 2 cups white vinegar
- 8 cups water
- 1 tablespoon sea salt
- 7 drops lemon essential oil
- 7 drops rosemary essential oil
- 1 tablespoon dried rosemary
- 1 tablespoon dried thyme

Combine all ingredients in a bucket, stirring clockwise while visualizing brilliant white light infusing the mixture. State your intention: "With this wash, all negativity dissolves, all stagnation clears, all spaces purify." Let herbs infuse for one hour, then strain before use.

Purification Spray:
- 1 cup witch hazel or high-proof vodka
- 1 cup spring or distilled water

- 7 drops each: rosemary, lemon, and pine essential oils
- 1 small clear quartz crystal

Combine liquid ingredients in a glass spray bottle. Add essential oils and place the cleansed crystal in the bottle. Shake well while visualizing purifying white light filling the mixture. Label and set in sunlight for several hours before use.

Preparation:

1 Begin by physically cleaning your home—clearing clutter, dusting, vacuuming, and opening windows briefly to establish air circulation.

2 Create sacred space by lighting the white candle in the center of your home and stating your intention: "I light this flame to illuminate all shadows and purify all spaces."

3 Place the bowl of salt near the candle as a grounding anchor for the ritual.

Ritual Process:

1 Begin at your front door, moving clockwise through your home.

2 First sound clearing: Ring bell, chime, or singing bowl in each corner of every room, moving from floor to ceiling. The vibration dislodges stagnant energy.

3 Smoke purification: Light your herbal bundle and allow it to smolder (not flame). Starting again at the front door, move clockwise through each room, focusing on:

- Corners where energy stagnates
- Doorways and windows where energy enters
- Electronic devices that generate electromagnetic fields
- Areas of previous conflict or heaviness

4 As you work, state: "With sacred smoke, I purify this space. All that does not serve departs now in peace."

5 Extinguish the herb bundle completely when finished.

6 Floor wash application: Beginning again at the front door, work backward toward the center of your home, washing thresholds, corners, and any areas that felt particularly heavy during smoke cleansing. As you clean, visualize negativity dissolving into the wash water.

7 Spray purification: After surfaces have dried, use your spray to mist the air in each room, focusing on areas that might have been missed by the smoke—inside closets, cabinets, and around delicate items that couldn't be exposed to smoke.

8 Final sound clearing: Complete with a second ringing of your bell or singing bowl, this time moving counterclockwise from the center of your home to the front door, pushing any remaining dislodged energy completely out of your space.

Sealing and Blessing:

1 Return to the center where your candle burns.

2 Dip your finger in the salt and trace a small protective symbol on each main window and door.

3 Place your fresh flowers or living plant in a central location, stating: "With new life, I establish fresh, positive energy in this cleansed space."

4 Wrap a small amount of unused salt in the white cloth and place it near your front door as an ongoing protective anchor.

5 Allow the candle to burn completely in a safe container to complete the purification process.

Maintenance: To maintain the purification, spritz entryways with your herb spray weekly and place small sachets of protective herbs (rosemary, garden sage, and bay leaf) in corners of primary living areas. Renew these sachets monthly at the new moon.

Timing Considerations: This ritual is most effective when performed during the waning moon for maximum banishing power. Dawn or dusk provide powerful transitional energy, while noon brings solar purification strength. Avoid performing during Mercury retrograde periods when energy tends to recirculate rather than depart cleanly.

Personal purification rituals prepare practitioners themselves for magical work, clearing accumulated energetic residue while establishing appropriate magical consciousness. Herbal baths provide immersive cleansing that simultaneously removes unwanted energetic attachments and imparts specific beneficial properties from the selected herbs. Smoke cleansing of the personal aura using appropriate herbal bundles quickly removes surface energetic contamination. Herbal scrubs combining salt or sugar with appropriate essential oils physically exfoliate while energetically removing stagnant or negative energy from the skin barrier. These personal purifications create clean energetic states ready for subsequent magical operations or serving as protection during challenging energy exchanges.

Ritual tools require regular purification to maintain magical efficacy, with herbs providing ideal cleansing agents specifically matched to tool functions. Crystal cleansing using dried herb bundles removes accumulated energetic imprints without water exposure that might damage certain stone types. Ritual blade purification traditionally uses smoke from protective herbs like rosemary or juniper to clear the tool while simultaneously strengthening its boundaries. Cleansing magical jewelry with herbal sachets or smoke removes energetic residue from public wearing while renewing protective or specific magical properties. These targeted tool cleansings maintain magical functionality while preventing cross-contamination between different magical operations.

Purification protocol development enables practitioners to create standardized cleansing procedures specifically designed for their personal practice. Effective protocols establish clear triggers for purification—after specific magical operations, following emotionally intense events, at regular calendar intervals, or when intuition indicates accumulating energetic debris. These personalized systems include appropriate herbal selections for different purification needs, proportional responses based on contamination levels, and clear completion markers that indicate when sufficient cleansing has occurred. Developing these systematic approaches ensures consistent magical hygiene while providing efficient responses to varied cleansing needs.

HERBS FOR LIFE TRANSITIONS AND RITES OF PASSAGE

Throughout human history, significant life transitions have been marked by formal ceremonies that acknowledge, support, and celebrate these pivotal moments. Herbal allies have traditionally played essential roles in these rites of passage, providing both symbolic representation of the transition and practical support for the energetic and emotional shifts involved. Contemporary green witches continue this tradition by creating meaningful ceremonies with appropriate herbal components to honor important life changes and support those experiencing them.

Herbal support for major transitions works through multiple simultaneous channels. Physically, properly selected herbs can address common symptoms experienced during life changes—calming nervous tension, supporting healthy sleep during stressful periods, or providing energy for demanding transition work. Energetically, herbs create bridges between states of being, facilitating smoother transitions between identities, roles, or life phases. Spiritually, ceremonial herb use connects contemporary transitions to timeless human experience, placing individual passages within larger contexts of meaning and purpose. This multi-level support creates comprehensive assistance for navigating significant life changes with grace and consciousness.

Herbal transition baths create powerful ceremonial vessels for marking important life changes through symbolic immersion. These ritual baths combine physical cleansing with energetic transformation, using water as both practical medium and magical representation of the liminal space between states. Herbs selected for transition baths typically include those that support release of previous states (such as bitter herbs for letting go), those that provide protection during vulnerable transition periods (protective aromatic herbs), and those that welcome or invoke desired new states (attractive, sweet-scented flowers). This three-part herbal formula creates a complete transitional container supporting the full arc of change from release through transition to new beginning.

Transition Bath: Career Change Ritual
Magical Purpose: Supports the energetic shift from a former career identity to a new professional path, releasing attachments to previous work while opening to new opportunities and avoiding career identity gaps during transition.
Appropriate For:
• Retirement transitions
• Major career changes
• Leaving toxic work environments
• Beginning entrepreneurial ventures
• Returning to work after extended absence

Herbal Components: *For Release (1 part):*
• Dandelion leaves (breaking through barriers, releasing established patterns)
• Burdock root pieces (pulling out deep attachments)
• Pine needles (releasing guilt about career changes)
• Blackberry leaves (cutting ties with appropriate boundaries)

For Protection During Transition (2 parts):
• Rosemary (mental clarity during uncertain periods)
• Basil (attracting prosperity during job transitions)
• Thyme (courage facing new challenges)
• Bay leaves (victory over professional obstacles)

For New Beginning (1 part):
• Cinnamon chips (accelerating new opportunities)
• Orange peel (optimism and enthusiasm)

- Ginger pieces (energizing new beginnings)
- Chamomile flowers (patience during development phases)

Additional Materials:
- White candle
- Journal and pen
- Small piece of paper
- Object representing former career
- Object representing new career direction
- Towel in color representing new career energy

Preparation:

1 Create a bundle with all herbs mixed together, or divide into three separate bundles (release, protection, new beginning) for a three-stage bath.

2 Place herbs in a large muslin bag or cheesecloth tied securely.

3 Fill bathtub with comfortably warm water.

4 Create sacred space in your bathroom through cleansing and boundary setting.

5 Light the white candle safely near the bath.

6 Place career objects where they can be seen but not submerged.

Ritual Bath Process:

Opening:

1 Stand before the bath and state your intention: "I stand at the threshold between professional identities. I honor the work I have completed and the knowledge gained. I now prepare to release what no longer serves my path And open to new professional growth and opportunity."

2 Write on the small paper one sentence about what you're

releasing from your former career and one sentence about what you're calling in for your new direction.

Release Phase:

1 If using separate bundles, place the release herb bundle in the bath first.

2 Enter the bath mindfully, visualizing yourself crossing a threshold.

3 Submerge as completely as comfortable, stating: "I release attachment to my former professional identity. I release expectations about career progression. I release fears of the unknown professional path."

4 Use the herb bundle to scrub your body from head to feet, moving downward to symbolize releasing energy into the water.

Transition Protection:

1 If using separate bundles, add the protection herbs now.

2 Cup water in your hands and pour it over your head three times, stating: "I remain protected during this career transition. My skills and knowledge remain intact and valuable. My professional worth exists independent of any job title."

3 Float in the water if possible, experiencing the sensation of being supported during uncertainty.

New Beginning:

1 If using separate bundles, add the new beginning herbs now.

2 Touch your heart center, solar plexus, and forehead with water infused with herbs, stating: "I open my heart to new professional passion. I empower my will to create new career success. I align my vision with my authentic professional purpose."

3 Visualize yourself surrounded by a color representing your new career direction.

Completion:

1 When ready, stand and allow the water to drip from your body, each drop carrying away old professional limitations.
2 Exit the bath and wrap yourself in the towel chosen to represent new career energy.
3 Light your paper from the candle and let it burn in a fireproof container, transforming written intentions through fire.
4 Write three immediate, practical steps for your career transition in your journal.

Follow-up Practice: Place a small jar of the dried herb mixture on your workspace or desk, reminding you of this transition ritual. Each morning for the next week, touch the jar briefly while affirming: "I am successfully navigating my career transition with confidence and clarity."

Ceremony design for major life events requires thoughtful consideration of multiple factors to create meaningful, effective rituals. The emotional state of participants significantly impacts appropriate herbal selection—those experiencing grief require gentle, supportive herbs rather than stimulating or challenging plants, while those celebrating joyful transitions benefit from expansive, expressive herbal allies. The desire for privacy or community involvement determines ritual structure—private ceremonies might focus on personal herbal applications like baths or anointings, while community rituals utilize shared herbal elements like incense, communal tea, or botanical decorations. Timing considerations align ceremonies with supportive natural cycles—waxing moon transitions emphasize growth and expansion, while waning moon ceremonies support release and completion. These design elements combine to create rituals precisely tailored to specific transition needs.

Coming-of-age ceremonies support young people transitioning to adult community roles, with herbs traditionally playing significant roles in these important rituals. Herbal components typically emphasize responsibility, wisdom development, and connection to ancestral knowledge. Cedar or juniper smoke cleansing opens ceremonies with purification that simultaneously connects to ancestral traditions. Protective herb pouches containing sage, rosemary, and appropriate local herbs provide ongoing support during the often challenging transition period. Oak leaves or acorns represent strength and enduring wisdom developing from small beginnings. These botanical elements connect contemporary coming-of-age experiences to timeless human transitions while providing practical support for the significant energetic changes involved.

Grief support rituals address the profound transitions following significant losses, with herbs providing gentle, compassionate assistance during these vulnerable passages. Rosemary has traditionally supported remembrance while providing protective boundaries during bereavement. Lavender offers calming properties that assist with the often overwhelming emotional waves accompanying grief. Roses support heart healing while honoring the beauty of what has been lost. Lemon balm gently uplifts without forcing premature happiness. These compassionate herbal allies create containers for authentic grief expression while preventing energetic depletion during intensive emotional processing.

SEASONAL HERBAL ALTAR PRACTICES

Altar creation represents one of the most fundamental and versatile magical practices, establishing focused sacred space for specific intentions, beings, or energies. Herbal components play essential roles in effective altar construction, providing physical anchors for particular magical properties while establishing sensory connections through appearance, texture, and aroma. By developing seasonal altar practices that evolve throughout the yearly cycle, practitioners create ongoing relationships with botanical allies while maintaining conscious connection to natural rhythms and energetic tides.

Altar fundamentals establish essential frameworks for effective ritual space. The physical altar structure—whether elaborate permanent installation or simple portable surface—creates the literal foundation for magical focus. Directional correspondences traditionally align altar components with their associated elements and qualities: east (air, communication, dawn), south (fire, transformation, noon), west (water, emotion, dusk), and north (earth, stability, midnight). Elemental representations provide both magical balance and access to specific elemental powers when needed. Personal altar styles range from minimalist designs with few essential items to elaborate constructions with numerous magical tools and representations. These fundamental considerations create coherent, balanced altar spaces capable of supporting various magical operations.

Seasonal rotation maintains altar relevance throughout the yearly cycle, connecting magical practice to immediate environmental conditions and energetic currents. Altar herbs ideally include both preserved botanicals from previous seasons and fresh specimens currently available, creating temporal continuity through plant relationships. Spring altars feature early flowers, emerging leaves, and sprouting seeds representing new beginnings and fresh growth. Summer installations showcase abundant flowers, lush foliage, and initial fruits symbolizing manifestation and fulfillment. Autumn altars incorporate harvest elements, seeds, nuts, and late fruits representing completion and preparation for inward turning. Winter arrangements utilize evergreens, dried herbs, roots, and dormant bulbs symbolizing hidden potential and inner work during apparent stillness. This continuous rotation creates year-round connection to natural cycles through intentional botanical relationships.

Seasonal Altar Guide: Summer Solstice
Magical Purpose: Creates a focused sacred space honoring peak solar energy, abundance manifestation, and the height of external power before the gradual return toward darkness.
Timing: Establish the summer solstice altar several days before the actual solstice to build energy, maintaining it for 7-9 days total (including solstice day) to fully work with the potent transitional period.
Directional Components:

East (Air/Dawn):
- Fresh lemon balm sprigs in water (joy, success)
- Yellow candle (illumination, mental clarity)
- Feather or representation of air element
- Small bell or chime

South (Fire/Noon):
- St. John's Wort flowers (traditional solstice herb)
- Sunflower or representation of the sun
- Red or gold candle (larger than others)
- Representation of fire element

West (Water/Dusk):
- Fresh roses in water (fulfillment, beauty at peak)
- Blue or sea-green candle
- Shell or representation of water element
- Small bowl of moon-charged water

North (Earth/Midnight):
- Early summer fruits and vegetables
- Green candle
- Stones or crystals (citrine, carnelian, or clear quartz)
- Representation of earth element

Central Focus:
- Solar symbol (wheel, spiral, or sun image)
- Gold or yellow altar cloth
- Oak leaves and/or acorns (traditional solstice symbols)
- Calendula flowers (solar representation)

Herbal Components and Arrangements:

Solar Herb Bundle: Create a bound bundle of solar herbs to hang above the altar or place in the center:

- St. John's Wort flowering tops (traditional solstice herb)
- Calendula flowers (solar tracking, healing)
- Lavender sprigs (peace during power)
- Rosemary (remembrance, protection)
- Bay leaves (victory, strength)
- Bind with gold or red thread

Fresh Flowers: Place vases or jars of fresh seasonal flowers appropriate to your region, focusing on sun-colored blooms (yellow, orange, red) and those that track the sun:
- Sunflowers
- Daisies
- Black-eyed Susans
- Marigolds
- California poppies

Herbal Offering Bowl: Create a small offering of herbs specifically gathered at dawn on the solstice itself:
- 3 perfect leaves from different plants
- 3 flowers of different colors
- 3 sprigs of aromatic herbs
- Place on a special dish with a small piece of honeycomb

Ritual Activation:

1 Establish the altar at dawn or noon in the days preceding the solstice.
2 Cleanse the space with sun-associated incense (frankincense, copal, or bay leaf).
3 Place each element mindfully, stating its purpose and connection to the solstice.

4 Light candles from east to south to west to north, acknowledging each direction.

5 Activate the central solar symbol by anointing it with sun-infused oil while stating: "At this pinnacle of light and power, At this moment of greatest solar strength, I honor the height of manifestation and growth. From this peak, I gather light to carry forward."

Daily Practices: Each day the altar remains active, perform at least one of these practices:

- Dawn connection: Light the eastern candle at sunrise with a brief gratitude statement
- Noon power ritual: Light the southern candle at midday, spending several minutes in meditation on your manifesting power
- Sunset acknowledgment: Light the western candle at sunset, recognizing the beginning of light's decline
- Evening reflection: Light the northern candle after dark, considering what harvest will come from current growth

Solstice Day Special Observance: On the actual solstice, refresh all herbal components early in the morning. Spend time at each cardinal point of the day (dawn, noon, sunset, midnight) with the altar, performing a special observance at solar noon:

1 Light all candles in clockwise order
2 Place the fresh herbal offering in the center
3 State your gratitude for peak light and energy
4 Acknowledge the wheel's turning toward eventual darkness
5 Set intentions for what you will manifest through the coming decrease

Dismantling Process: When the altar period concludes, mindfully dismantle in reverse order of creation, thanking each element and direction. Take the central herbal bundle and hang it in your home to carry solstice energy forward. Compost fresh plant material with gratitude, or dry special components for use in future magical work throughout the year.

Adaptations:
• Apartment practitioners can create miniature versions using small potted plants
• Southern hemisphere practitioners should invert the entire concept to honor winter solstice
• Regional variations should incorporate locally significant plants associated with peak summer

Working altar practices maintain active relationship with established sacred space through regular engagement and offering practices. Daily acknowledgments—lighting candles at specific times, refreshing water offerings, or adding incense—establish consistent magical attention that maintains altar potency. Weekly refreshing of herbal components—replacing wilted flowers, adding seasonal botanicals, or rearranging existing elements—keeps the altar energetically vital while demonstrating ongoing commitment to the relationship. Monthly deep cleaning—removing all items, cleansing the altar surface, and intentionally replacing each component—prevents energetic stagnation while providing opportunities for reassessing magical focus. These maintenance practices transform altars from static displays into living magical tools with ongoing relevance and power.

Ritual utilization transforms static altar arrangements into active magical technology. Pre-ritual activation using appropriate herbal incense, sprays, or sounds prepares altar space for specific magical operations. Focused magical work directly involving altar components—lighting specific directional candles for particular purposes, activating herbal representatives through touch or breath, or arranging components in specific patterns—channels altar energy toward intended outcomes. Post-ritual acknowledgment through gratitude offerings, candle extinguishing rituals, or closing gestures completes energy cycles while maintaining respectful relationship with altar components. These utilization practices transform decorative arrangements into functional magical instruments capable of supporting varied operations.

Through these herbal cleansing rituals, transition ceremonies, and seasonal altar practices, practitioners develop sophisticated magical operations that address specific needs with comprehensive herbal support. These structured workings create containers for transformation, healing, and celebration while maintaining conscious connection to natural cycles and botanical allies. By mastering these ritual frameworks, green witches develop the ability to design and perform powerful ceremonies tailored to particular magical requirements, expanding herbal practice beyond individual applications into complete, integrated magical systems.

CHAPTER 11

HEALING APPLICATIONS OF MAGICAL HERBALISM

Healing represents one of the oldest and most essential applications of herbal magic, bridging the often artificial divide between magical practice and practical medicine. Throughout history, effective healers have addressed health on multiple simultaneous levels—physical symptoms, emotional imbalances, spiritual disconnections, and energetic disruptions. Contemporary magical herbalism continues this holistic tradition, recognizing that complete healing requires attending to the whole person rather than isolated symptoms. This chapter explores three essential aspects of herbal healing magic: emergency magical first aid, emotional and psychological support, and spiritual cleansing baths that address healing needs across multiple dimensions of being.

CREATING A MAGICAL HERBAL FIRST AID KIT

The magical first aid kit represents a sophisticated healing tool that addresses both immediate physical concerns and the subtle energetic, emotional, and spiritual aspects that accompany injury or illness. Unlike conventional first aid supplies that focus exclusively on physical symptoms, the witch's healing kit provides comprehensive support for the whole person experiencing distress. By thoughtfully assembling, empowering, and maintaining such a kit, practitioners create a practical magical tool for responding effectively to various healing emergencies.

Kit construction begins with container selection and preparation. Choose a container that balances practical considerations—durability, appropriate size, water-resistance—with magical correspondences supporting healing intentions. Traditional wooden boxes bring Earth energy for grounding and stability during crisis, while metal containers provide protective boundaries that prevent energy leakage. Whatever material you select, thoroughly cleanse the container both physically and energetically before assembly. Create formal magical boundaries through clear intention setting, defining both what the kit will address and what falls outside its intended scope. This boundary setting focuses the kit's energy while preventing magical diffusion that might reduce effectiveness.

Physical supplies form the practical foundation of any effective first aid kit. Include basic conventional items—bandages, antiseptic wipes, tweezers, gloves, tape, and scissors

—as these address immediate physical needs that often accompany magical healing requirements. Add relevant herbal preparations in forms supporting emergency use—tinctures for rapid effects, salves for topical application, powders for sprinkling or mixing, and small vials of essential oils for aromatic applications. Include tools for administering these preparations—droppers, small measuring cups, cotton pads, and application tools. These physical components enable prompt, practical response to healing needs while serving as vehicles for magical healing influences.

Herbal selection balances versatility with targeted efficacy, focusing on plant allies that address common emergency needs while offering multiple application options. Yarrow serves as a primary emergency ally, with remarkable hemostatic properties for wound treatment alongside energetic abilities to repair torn subtle bodies and etheric damage. Lavender provides antimicrobial properties for physical cleansing while simultaneously calming panic and restoring emotional equilibrium during crisis. Echinacea supports immune response against potential infection while energetically reinforcing protective boundaries against opportunistic energy drains during vulnerability. St. John's Wort offers both antibiotic action for wound care and solar protective energy against negative subtle influences that might exploit openings created by injury. These multifunctional herbs maximize kit effectiveness while maintaining reasonable size and complexity.

Magical First Aid Kit: Core Herbal Components

Yarrow (Achillea millefolium) *Physical Applications:* Hemostatic for wound treatment, antimicrobial for infection prevention *Magical Functions:* Seals energetic leaks, repairs damage to subtle bodies, establishes appropriate boundaries

Preparation Forms:
- Powdered dried herb in sealed container for direct wound application
- Strong tincture (1:3 extraction) for internal and external use
- Infused oil for wound dressing
- Small bundle of dried herb for emergency smudging of affected areas

Emergency Usage Instructions: For bleeding wounds with energetic disruption:

1 Apply physical pressure using clean cloth
2 Sprinkle small amount of yarrow powder directly on wound while stating: "As yarrow seals this physical wound, so it repairs all subtle bodies and energetic fields."
3 Once bleeding slows, apply 3-5 drops of yarrow tincture around (not in) the wound in a clockwise circle
4 Dress wound with conventional bandage
5 Administer 3 drops of tincture in water internally while visualizing complete energetic repair
6 For lingering energetic disruption, pass the dried herb bundle through candle flame and use the smoke to cleanse the affected area and surrounding energy field

Lavender (Lavandula angustifolia) *Physical Applications:* Antimicrobial, analgesic, mild sedative *Magical Functions:*

Calms emotional distress, restores equilibrium, purifies negative influences

Preparation Forms:
- Essential oil (therapeutic grade only) in amber glass with orifice reducer
- Dried flowers in sealed container
- Hydrosol in spray bottle
- Infused honey for internal stress support

Emergency Usage Instructions: For panic attacks with physical manifestations:

1 Apply one drop of lavender oil to each temple while stating: "Peace flows through all levels of being, restoring natural calm and balance."
2 Spray hydrosol in a counterclockwise circle around the affected person, creating a boundary of protected space
3 Place dried flowers in the person's hands to hold and focus on, engaging sensory awareness to ground scattered energy
4 Administer half teaspoon of lavender honey under the tongue for internal support
5 Guide three deep breaths with inhale through nose (directly smelling lavender in hands) and exhale through mouth
6 Repeat as needed until equilibrium returns

Echinacea (Echinacea purpurea/angustifolia) *Physical Applications:* Immune enhancement, lymphatic support, mild antibiotic *Magical Functions:* Strengthens energetic immunity, prevents psychic infection, creates resilient boundaries

Preparation Forms:
- Potent tincture (fresh root and flower 1:2 extraction)

- Dried root pieces for emergency decoction
- Powdered root in capsules for internal support
- Flower essence for energetic boundary work

Emergency Usage Instructions: For exposure to contagious illness with energetic vulnerability:

1 Administer 30 drops of tincture in water immediately, stating: "Physical and energetic immunity strengthen now, creating resilient protection on all levels."

2 Place one drop of flower essence on the crown chakra, third eye, throat, and heart

3 Create protective circle by sprinkling small amount of powdered root around the person

4 Repeat tincture in diminishing doses (20 drops, then 10 drops) at 30-minute intervals

5 For ongoing protection, prepare capsules to be taken three times daily while maintaining visualization of a purple protective field surrounding the body

St. John's Wort (Hypericum perforatum) *Physical Applications:* Analgesic, anti-inflammatory, antiviral, wound healing *Magical Functions:* Solar protection, dispels negativity, mends energy body trauma

Preparation Forms:
- Red infused oil (solar prepared) for external application
- Tincture for internal and external use
- Dried flowering tops for infusion
- Flower essence for subtle body repair

Emergency Usage Instructions: For nerve damage with concurrent energy body injury:

HEALING APPLICATIONS OF MAGICAL HERBALISM

1 Apply infused oil gently to affected area, moving in sunwise (clockwise) direction while stating: "Solar light heals all damaged tissues, physical and subtle."
2 Place 5 drops of tincture in water and administer internally
3 Create rapid infusion by steeping dried herb in hot water for 7 minutes, strain, and use as wash for affected area
4 Apply 4 drops of flower essence to solar plexus
5 If outdoors, position affected area in direct sunlight briefly while visualizing golden light penetrating through all levels of being
6 For ongoing support, repeat applications at sunrise, noon, and sunset for three consecutive days

Energetic components extend the kit's effectiveness beyond physical remedies to address subtle aspects of healing emergencies. Charged crystals provide stable energetic templates supporting various healing needs—clear quartz for energy amplification, amethyst for pain relief and calming, smoky quartz for grounding during shock, and rose quartz for heart support during emotional trauma. A dedicated emergency candle, preferably white or blue, creates immediate sacred space when lit, establishing a protective perimeter for healing work. Emergency essence combinations in dropper bottles provide rapid subtle body support, particularly valuable when physical remedies require time to take effect. Small protection talismans offer energetic shields that prevent further negative influences from affecting vulnerable individuals during healing processes. These energetic tools complement herbal components by addressing invisible aspects of healing needs.

Kit activation transforms assembled components into a cohesive magical tool greater than the sum of its parts. Once all elements are gathered, perform a formal integration ritual —connecting components through shared intention, establishing communication pathways between different elements, and programming the complete kit for rapid response to emergency needs. Create activation symbols on the container itself, representing healing, protection, and rapid effectiveness. Establish verbal activation phrases or gestures that instantly engage the kit's full magical potential when needed. These activation elements transform individual supplies into a unified magical instrument ready for immediate deployment.

Maintenance ensures continued effectiveness through both practical upkeep and energetic renewal. Regularly check physical supplies for expiration dates, degradation, or depletion, replacing items as needed to maintain complete readiness. Perform seasonal energetic refreshing corresponding to natural healing energies—spring cleansing for renewal properties, summer solstice recharging for maximum power, autumn balancing for homeostasis, and winter quiet maintenance for deep healing potential. Recharge crystals according to their specific needs and cleanse any components that have absorbed significant negative energy during use. This regular maintenance creates a perpetually ready magical tool while deepening your relationship with the healing allies contained within the kit.

HERBS FOR EMOTIONAL AND PSYCHOLOGICAL SUPPORT

Emotional and psychological healing represents one of herbalism's most valuable contributions to holistic wellness. While conventional approaches often artificially separate physical symptoms from emotional states, magical herbalism recognizes their intrinsic connection, addressing emotional needs with the same seriousness and sophistication applied to physical concerns. Herbal allies offer powerful support for navigating challenging emotional landscapes, processing psychological difficulties, and maintaining mental wellness through life's inevitable transitions.

Emotional first aid provides immediate support during acute emotional distress, offering herbal allies that facilitate stabilization and initial healing. Rose offers heart-centered comfort during grief and heartbreak, creating safe emotional containers for processing profound loss. Lemon balm brings gentle uplifting energy during depression without forcing artificial happiness, respecting the authentic emotional process while preventing dangerous downward spirals. Skullcap calms anxiety and panic through direct nervous system support, creating space for rational assessment during overwhelming emotional states. These emergency interventions establish foundations for deeper healing work once immediate emotional crises stabilize.

Emotional Emergency Formula: Acute Grief Support
Magical Purpose: Provides immediate support during the

first stages of significant loss, creating a compassionate container for grief while preventing dangerous emotional shock and energetic collapse.

Appropriate For:
- Death of loved ones
- Relationship endings
- Significant life losses (home, career, health)
- Traumatic disappointments
- Unexpected major life changes

Formula Components: *Base Support (60%):*
- Rose petals or rose glycerite (heart holding, emotional containment)
- Hawthorn berries and flowers (heart strength, grief protection)
- Linden flowers (emotional softening without collapse)

Nervous System Stability (30%):
- Skullcap herb (prevents emotional overwhelm)
- Lavender flowers (calming without suppression)
- Milky oat tops (nourishment during emotional depletion)

Energy Protection (10%):
- Rosemary (boundaries, preventing energy depletion)
- Yarrow flowers (sealing energetic wounds from sudden severing)

Preparation Forms: This formula can be prepared in several forms depending on the situation:

Immediate Response Tincture:
- Prepare as 1:4 extraction in 50% alcohol
- Standard dose: 30-60 drops in small amount of water
- Acute dosing: 30 drops every 30 minutes for up to 4 doses

- Store in amber glass with dropper top

Supportive Tea:
- 1 teaspoon base support herbs
- ½ teaspoon nervous system herbs
- Pinch of protective herbs
- Steep covered for 15 minutes
- Add honey if desired (preferably rose-infused)
- Drink up to 3 cups daily during acute grief

Essence Spray:
- Combine tincture with equal parts rose water
- Add 7 drops rose essential oil per 2 oz
- Store in spray bottle for environmental support
- Spray around person, living space, and especially bedding

Administration with Magical Intention:

1 Before administering any form, hold the remedy between your palms and state: "This support creates safe space for natural grief while preventing harmful collapse. Emotions flow appropriately without overwhelming the heart or spirit."

2 For tincture: Place drops under the tongue while visualizing a soft pink light surrounding the heart center.

3 For tea: Ask the person to cup the tea in both hands before drinking, feeling its warmth as supportive presence.

4 For spray: Move around the person in a clockwise direction, creating a protective energy field while spraying.

Supporting Magic:
- Place a small rose quartz near the person while they sleep
- Create a simple altar with a white candle and photo or symbol of what was lost

- Suggest writing unsent letters to express emotions, burning them in a safe container afterward
- Provide a small sachet of the dry formula to carry during difficult days

Duration Guidelines: Acute formula is appropriate for the first 2-4 weeks of grief. For longer support, transition to a grief processing formula with different proportions (more rose, less protective herbs) to facilitate healthy emotional movement through the grief process rather than containment.

Cautions: This formula supports natural grief but is not appropriate for clinical depression requiring professional intervention. The presence of suicidal thoughts, inability to perform basic self-care, or complete emotional shutdown requires immediate professional support.

Long-term emotional healing requires different herbal approaches than acute intervention, focusing on sustained balance and gradual transformation rather than immediate relief. Mimosa bark (Albizia julibrissin) provides gentle heart healing and emotional resilience for extended grief recovery, traditionally called "collective happiness bark" for its ability to restore joy without denying emotional depth. Holy basil builds adaptive capacity for navigating ongoing stress, enhancing resilience while maintaining appropriate emotional responsiveness. Milky oats offer deep nervous system restoration during extended emotional challenges, literally rebuilding depleted resources rather than simply masking exhaustion. These long-term allies work best when used consistently over time, gradually shifting emotional patterns rather than forcing immediate change.

Ritual approaches enhance herbal effectiveness for emotional healing by creating meaningful containers for psychological processing. Dream pillows combining appropriate herbs with intention-setting support emotional processing during sleep states when conscious resistance diminishes. Ceremonial teas consumed with specific mindfulness practices create designated time for emotional attention often neglected in busy lives. Symbolic herbal baths marking emotional transitions—releasing relationships, completing grief work, or acknowledging psychological growth—create tangible experiences of emotional movement that combat stagnation. These ritual dimensions transform simple herbal consumption into sacred healing practice, engaging multiple aspects of being in the emotional healing process.

Professional support integration maintains ethical boundaries while maximizing healing effectiveness. Responsible herbal practice recognizes appropriate limitations, with practitioners clearly distinguishing between general emotional support and treatment of diagnosed mental health conditions requiring professional care. Collaborative approaches often prove most effective—herbal allies supporting therapy processes, magical practices enhancing psychiatric treatment, or energy work complementing psychological counseling. These integrated approaches honor both traditional healing wisdom and contemporary psychological understanding, creating comprehensive support systems for complex emotional healing needs.

SPIRITUAL CLEANSING AND PROTECTIVE HERBAL BATHS

Bathing transcends simple physical cleansing to become a powerful vehicle for spiritual healing across numerous magical traditions. The combination of water's receptivity, herbs' specific magical properties, and the liminal nature of immersion creates ideal conditions for profound spiritual cleansing, protection establishment, and energetic renewal. By understanding the principles and practices of magical bathing, practitioners access one of the most universally effective methods for spiritual healing and maintenance.

Bath construction follows specific principles that enhance magical effectiveness. Water temperature influences magical properties—hot water opens energy bodies and promotes release, while cool water tones and strengthens energetic boundaries. Water sources carry inherent magical signatures—rainwater brings transformative qualities, spring water offers vitality and renewal, ocean water provides deep cleansing and ancestral connection. Herbal selection combines primary herbs addressing the specific spiritual healing needed with supporting herbs that direct and enhance the primary action. Additive elements—salts, clays, milk, honey, or oils—contribute additional magical properties while influencing how herbal properties interact with both water and the bather's energy field. These construction elements combine to create precisely targeted magical tools for specific spiritual healing needs.

Spiritual Cleansing Bath: Negative Attachment Release

Magical Purpose: Removes unwanted spiritual attachments, psychic cords, negative thought forms, and unhealthy energetic connections while strengthening natural spiritual boundaries.

Appropriate For:
- After unhealthy relationship endings
- Following spiritual healing work performed on others
- After spending time in energetically contaminated environments
- When experiencing persistent energy drainage
- During spiritual intrusion or unwanted psychic contact

Bath Components:

Primary Cleansing Herbs (2 parts):
- Hyssop (powerful spiritual cleanser across traditions)
- Rue (cuts unhealthy bonds, particularly effective against hexes)
- Pine needles (dissolves negative attachments)
- Angelica root (protection against spiritual entities)

Boundary Restoration Herbs (1 part):
- Rosemary (strong boundary establishment)
- Thyme (courage during spiritual clearing)
- Bay leaves (victory over spiritual intrusions)

Energetic Support Herbs (1 part):
- Rose petals (heart protection during release)
- Lavender (calm during potentially intense cleansing)
- Lemon balm (joy restoration in cleared spaces)

Additional Elements:

- Sea salt or black salt (2 cups minimum)
- Apple cider vinegar (1 cup)
- Lemon juice (from one fresh lemon)
- White or blue candle
- Matches or lighter
- Towel (preferably white)
- Fresh clothes that have been cleansed and blessed

Preparation Timing: Prepare during the waning moon, ideally on a Saturday (Saturn's day for boundaries) or Tuesday (Mars' day for cutting connections). The hour after sunset provides natural transition energy supporting release work.

Bath Preparation:

1 Begin by physically cleaning your bathroom space, paying special attention to removing any residual energies through appropriate cleansing methods.

2 Fill the bathtub with comfortably warm water (slightly warmer than body temperature to open energy bodies).

3 Create a strong herbal infusion:
- Combine all herbs in a large pot
- Add 8 cups of water
- Bring to a boil, then reduce heat
- Simmer covered for 20 minutes
- Turn off heat and steep an additional 20 minutes
- Strain directly into the bathwater

4 Add in sequence, stirring clockwise with your hand or a wooden spoon:
- Sea salt or black salt, stating: "By salt's power, all negativity dissolves."

HEALING APPLICATIONS OF MAGICAL HERBALISM

- Apple cider vinegar, stating: "By vinegar's sharpness, all cords are cut."
- Lemon juice, squeezed directly into water, stating: "By lemon's clarity, all is purified."

5 Place and light the candle safely near the bath, stating: "This light illuminates all hidden attachments and guides their complete release."

Bathing Ritual:

1 Before entering the bath, stand before it and set clear intention: "I now release all energetic attachments that do not serve my highest good. I reclaim my personal power from all external sources. I restore my natural spiritual boundaries to full integrity."

2 Enter the bath mindfully, fully immersing if possible while stating: "As water surrounds me, all negative connections dissolve. What is not mine returns to its source. What is mine returns purified to my being."

3 Beginning at your feet and working upward, use your hands to scrub your entire body with the herbal water, paying special attention to:

- Back of neck (common attachment point)
- Solar plexus (power center often drained)
- Lower back (vulnerability point)
- Wrists and ankles (binding points)

4 As you scrub each area, specifically name attachments you're releasing: "I release the energy cords from [specific relationship]." "I return the emotional burden of [specific situation]." "I clear the influence of [specific negative thought pattern]."

5 When complete, submerge fully if possible, holding breath briefly while visualizing all remaining attachments dissolving into the water.

6 Upon rising from full immersion, state firmly: "Cleansed, cleared, and restored to my sovereign energetic state. My boundaries are strong, my energy is my own. It is done."

7 Remain in the bath 5-10 more minutes, allowing the herbs to complete their work.

8 Exit the bath, allowing yourself to air dry if possible rather than using a towel, visualizing the last water drops carrying away final traces of unwanted connections.

Completion:

1 Dress in fresh, clean clothes that have not been worn during the problematic connection period.

2 Allow bathwater to drain completely while visualizing all negative attachments flowing away.

3 Rinse tub thoroughly with fresh water.

4 Spend the remainder of the evening in a protected, peaceful environment.

5 Avoid contact with sources of former attachments for at least 24 hours to allow new boundaries to strengthen.

Follow-up Practice: For three days following the bath, begin each morning by visualizing a complete egg of protective light surrounding your body. Each evening, perform a brief aura brush-down with your hands, sweeping from head to feet to remove any attempting reattachments.

Caution: Rue can cause skin irritation in sensitive individuals and is photosensitizing. If skin sensitivity is a concern, reduce rue proportion or keep bath water cooler. Avoid sun exposure immediately after bathing.

Traditional recipes from various cultural traditions offer tested formulations developed through generations of practical experience. Mexican baños de hierbas typically layer protective, cleansing, and blessing herbs to create comprehensive spiritual healing experiences. Hoodoo spiritual baths often employ specific numerical combinations (3, 7, 9, or 13 herbs) to create precisely targeted energetic effects. Brazilian banhos de descarrego emphasize powerful release properties through both herbal selection and specific bathing techniques. Caribbean spiritual baths frequently incorporate specific color associations and planetary timing to enhance effectiveness. These traditional approaches provide valuable foundations while allowing for adaptation to individual needs and locally available herbs.

Application methods significantly impact bath effectiveness. Full immersion provides comprehensive treatment but requires substantial herbal material and may prove impractical in some situations. Three-point washing—using specially prepared herbal waters to cleanse specific body points in particular sequences—offers targeted treatment using minimal materials. Foot baths concentrate on the grounding connection point with Earth energies while requiring less preparation than full baths. Steam treatments use herbal vapors to access respiratory systems and subtle energy centers in the head while conserving water and herbs. These varied applications allow practitioners to select methods proportional to specific healing needs while accommodating practical limitations.

Timing considerations enhance bath effectiveness by aligning with supportive natural cycles. Moon phases provide basic guidance—waxing moon for strengthening, building, and attracting; full moon for maximum power and illumination; waning moon for releasing, banishing, and diminishing; new moon for complete renewal and fresh beginnings. Planetary hours add further refinement—Mars hours for cutting cords and aggressive cleansing, Jupiter hours for expansive blessing, Venus hours for harmonious healing, Saturn hours for boundary establishment. Personal timing factors—significant anniversaries, personal power days, or individual biorhythms—further customize timing for maximum resonance with the individual receiving treatment. These temporal alignments create optimal conditions for effective spiritual bathing.

Through these healing applications—magical first aid, emotional support, and spiritual cleansing baths—practitioners develop comprehensive approaches to wellness that address the whole person rather than isolated symptoms. By combining traditional wisdom with contemporary understanding, the green witch creates healing modalities that honor the complex interconnection between physical, emotional, and spiritual aspects of human experience. This integrated approach represents one of magical herbalism's most valuable contributions to holistic healing arts—the recognition that true wellness emerges through balanced attention to all dimensions of being.

CHAPTER 12

ADVANCED HERBAL MAGIC TECHNIQUES

As practitioners deepen their relationships with plant allies and develop foundational skills, more sophisticated herbal magic techniques become accessible. This chapter explores advanced practices that extend beyond basic applications into specialized realms requiring greater sensitivity, skill, and discernment. These techniques—working with plant spirits and deities, dream and divination practices, and shamanic plant relationships—represent the deeper currents of herbal magic available to experienced practitioners. While these advanced practices require significant preparation and commitment, they offer profound magical partnerships and experiences that transform both practice and practitioner through direct engagement with plant consciousness and power.

WORKING WITH PLANT SPIRITS AND DEITIES

Beyond the physical and energetic properties of herbs lies the realm of plant spirits—the conscious intelligence residing within plant species. Throughout magical traditions worldwide, practitioners have recognized and engaged with these intelligences as distinct beings capable of communication, teaching, and collaborative magical work. Advanced herbal magic includes developing direct relationships with these plant spirits, creating ongoing partnerships that transcend simple utilization of herb properties and enter the realm of conscious cooperation with botanical intelligences.

Plant spirits manifest across a spectrum of consciousnesses, from the specific spirit of an individual plant to the overarching intelligence of an entire species, sometimes extending to plant deities who embody the archetypal power of particular botanical families or magical properties. Individual plant spirits offer the most direct and personal connections, particularly with plants you have grown from seed or tended for substantial time. Species spirits represent the collective consciousness and magical pattern of an entire plant type—Oak, Rose, or Mugwort as broad intelligences rather than single specimens. Plant deities embody the deepest archetypal aspects of plant magic, often appearing in traditional pantheons as gods or goddesses associated with particular plants or plant powers. These varied levels of plant consciousness offer different types of magical partnerships adapted to specific practitioner needs and affinities.

Initial contact with plant spirits requires clearing preconceptions while developing receptivity to non-human communication forms. Plants communicate primarily through direct impression rather than language—instantaneous knowing, symbolic imagery, bodily sensations, emotional shifts, or intuitive understanding. These communications rarely emerge as human-style conversations but rather as holistic transmissions that simultaneously convey multiple levels of meaning and experience. This communication style requires expanding awareness beyond verbal expectation while developing sensitivity to subtle impression and direct knowing. Regular meditative practice with specific plant allies gradually attunes perception to their particular communication frequencies and patterns.

Technique: Developing Plant Spirit Relationships
Purpose: Establishes direct, conscious connection with a specific plant spirit for teaching, magical partnership, and collaborative work beyond basic herb usage.
Preparation Requirements:
• At least 3-6 months previous experience working with the physical herb
• Thorough understanding of the plant's growth habits, traditional uses, and basic properties
• Location with an actual living specimen of the plant (ideally one you've grown or tended)
• Dedicated journal for recording plant communications
• Offerings appropriate to the specific plant
• Undisturbed time (minimum 30 minutes initially, extending with practice)

Selecting Your Initial Plant Ally: Begin with plants demonstrating these characteristics:
• Strong personal resonance and positive history of work together
• Noted in traditions for their teaching or communication abilities (examples: mugwort, tobacco, rose, dandelion)
• Currently growing and accessible in living form
• Non-toxic and without psychoactive properties for initial practice
• Plants already growing in your garden or home environment often make ideal first allies, as connection has already begun through physical proximity and care relationship

Preliminary Connection Protocol: Before attempting direct communication, establish relationship foundations:
1 Spend regular time in physical proximity to the plant without agenda—simply being present
2 Provide appropriate care—water, nutrition, support, protection—establishing reciprocity
3 Research traditional relationships with this plant across cultures
4 Work with the physical plant in multiple forms (tea, tincture, food, etc.) to understand its effects on your system
5 Notice when the plant appears in dreams, synchronicities, or unexpected thoughts
6 Begin speaking aloud to the plant during care, expressing gratitude and intention

First Formal Communication Session:
1 Choose appropriate timing—dawn and dusk offer natural thresholds favorable for cross-species communication

2 Bring appropriate offerings based on research and intuition:
- Water-loving plants: spring water, rain collection
- Flowering plants: honey, flower essences
- Protective plants: coins, protective stones
- Teaching plants: tobacco (where traditional and appropriate)

3 Approach the plant with clear respect, introducing yourself formally even if you have tended it for years

4 Present your offering with specific acknowledgment of what you appreciate about the plant

5 State your intention clearly: "I come seeking to establish clear communication and mutual relationship beyond physical usage."

6 Sit comfortably within the plant's energy field (ideally touching or very near)

7 Begin with breath alignment—visualize breathing in rhythm with the plant's own processes of respiration

8 Allow your consciousness to shift from verbal thinking to sensory awareness, particularly noting:
- Physical sensations in your body
- Emotional shifts or sudden feelings
- Images that appear in your mind's eye
- Knowing that arises without logical process

9 When impressions begin, acknowledge them with simple internal gratitude

10 For your first session, remain receptive without asking specific questions

11 Complete by expressing gratitude and stating when you will return

12 Immediately record all impressions in your journal without editing or rationalization

Developing Ongoing Relationship: Following initial contact, deepen the relationship through:

1 Regular communication sessions (at least weekly)
2 Incremental extension of communication duration
3 Gradual introduction of specific questions, beginning with those about the plant itself
4 Validation of received information through research and practical application
5 Reciprocal support—implementing guidance received while continuing physical care
6 Introduction of the plant ally to your magical practice through formal acknowledgment

Communication Troubleshooting: If connection seems blocked or unclear:

- Return to physical relationship basis—provide care, use the herb, spend time in proximity
- Check timing—some plants communicate more clearly in particular seasons or moon phases
- Examine expectations—human-style conversation rarely occurs; expect alternative communication forms
- Consider incompatibility—not every plant will become a primary ally; respect natural affinity patterns
- Evaluate readiness—some powerful plant teachers require preliminary work with gentler allies

Ethical Considerations:

- Plant spirit relationships involve mutual consent—respect communications indicating boundaries

- Relationships require reciprocity—ongoing exchange rather than one-way benefit
- Communications are primarily for mutual relationship rather than immediate magical utilization
- Information received may be meant for personal use rather than public sharing
- Traditional plant relationships within specific cultures deserve acknowledgment and respect

Plant deities represent a specialized aspect of plant spirit work, involving relationships with the most archetypal manifestations of plant consciousness. Unlike individual plant spirits, these deities embody entire categories of plant magic and often appear in traditional pantheons—Dionysus with grape and vine energy, Brighid with healing herbs, Pachamama with coca and earth plants. Working with these deities requires formal devotional practices alongside herbal connections—creating dedicated altar spaces, observing traditional offerings and observances, and developing relationships through established devotional frameworks. These relationships develop gradually through consistent attention and sincere engagement, sometimes requiring years of dedicated practice before deep connection manifests.

Offerings form essential components of plant spirit relationships, establishing reciprocity while demonstrating sincere engagement. Traditional offerings vary widely across cultures and individual plants—pure water serves many plants, while others traditionally receive tobacco, corn meal, honey, wine, or specific minerals. Research traditional offering practices while also developing discernment about culturally closed practices that should not be appropriated. Beyond physical offerings, reciprocity includes protection of plant habitats, ethical harvesting practices, seed saving and propagation, and personal lifestyle choices that support plant communities. These multifaceted offerings create balanced exchange relationships rather than exploitative interactions.

Regular alliance maintenance ensures ongoing effective relationships with plant spirits and deities. Establish consistent communication practices—daily acknowledgment, weekly deeper connection, and seasonal ceremonies marking significant points in the plant's growth cycle. Create dedicated altar spaces for primary plant allies, with physical representations, appropriate offerings, and regular attention. Integrate plant ally acknowledgment into broader magical practice through formal invocations before working with the physical herb. Document communications in dedicated journals, creating records of the developing relationship while demonstrating respect for received wisdom. These maintenance practices transform occasional interactions into true spiritual partnerships characterized by mutual benefit and ongoing evolution.

DREAM WORK AND DIVINATION WITH HERBS

Dreams offer direct access to subconscious knowledge and non-ordinary awareness, making dream space an ideal environment for deepening herbal relationships and receiving plant teachings. Similarly, divination creates intentional gateways to intuitive knowledge typically obscured by ordinary consciousness. Herbs support both these practices by enhancing natural psychic abilities, creating appropriate consciousness states, and providing specific magical correspondences that direct awareness toward particular information sources. Advanced practitioners develop sophisticated techniques for using herbs to access these altered awareness states for specific magical purposes.

Dream enhancement through herbal allies follows several distinct approaches, each supporting different types of dream work. Dream recall enhancement employs herbs like mugwort, lavender, and bay laurel to strengthen memory connections between dream and waking states without necessarily altering dream content. Dream vividness amplification uses mimosa bark, passionflower, or blue lotus to intensify dream experiences through increased sensory awareness and emotional engagement during dream states. Lucid dream facilitation employs herbs like hops, California poppy, or celastrus seed to maintain partial waking consciousness during dream experiences, allowing conscious direction of dream content. Prophetic dream support utilizes herbs traditionally associated with foresight—wormwood, yarrow, and star anise—to align dream content with divinatory purposes.

Dream Pillow: Ancestral Wisdom Connection

Magical Purpose: Creates a specialized dream tool for establishing communication with ancestral wisdom sources through enhanced dream states, particularly focused on receiving herbal knowledge held within family lineages.

Appropriate For:
- Seeking guidance from ancestors with herbal knowledge
- Recovering lost family healing traditions
- Reconnecting with cultural herbal practices
- Receiving direction for healing family patterns
- Establishing ongoing dream communication with ancestral guides

Herbal Components:

Dream Gateway Herbs (2 parts):
- Mugwort (Artemisia vulgaris) - primary dream gate opener
- Bay leaves (Laurus nobilis) - clarity of vision and prophecy
- Lavender (Lavandula angustifolia) - calming protection during dream journeys

Ancestral Connection Herbs (2 parts):
- Rose petals (Rosa spp.) - heart connection to lineage
- Rosemary (Rosmarinus officinalis) - remembrance and memory
- Oak moss (Evernia prunastri) - ancient wisdom, rootedness
- Cedar chips (Thuja spp.) - ancestral protection and guidance

Supportive Herbs (1 part):
- Chamomile (Matricaria chamomilla) - stress reduction for deeper sleep
- Hops (Humulus lupulus) - dream intensification
- Lemon balm (Melissa officinalis) - joyful communication

Personal Connection Elements:
- Small piece of fabric from family heirloom or cultural significance
- Tiny photograph or representation of specific ancestor (if seeking particular connection)

- Three strands of your own hair
- Small paper with written intention

Materials Needed:
- 5"x7" cotton or linen fabric in blue or purple (dream colors)
- Sewing supplies or strong fabric glue
- Cotton or silk stuffing material
- Small piece of paper and pen
- String in white or purple
- Moonstone, amethyst, or clear quartz (optional)

Timing: Create during the dark moon for deepest ancestral connection, or during the full moon for greatest clarity of communication. The hours between midnight and 3am (the deepest ancestral hours) are traditionally most potent for this work.

Preparation:

1 Begin by cleansing all materials through appropriate methods (smoke, moonlight, sound).
2 Create sacred space specifically invoking ancestral blessing and protection.
3 Prepare your herbs, grinding slightly to release aromatics while maintaining texture.
4 Mix all herb categories together while focusing on your ancestral lineage.
5 On the small paper, write clearly: "I open to dream wisdom from my ancestors of positive intention. I seek herbal knowledge for healing benefit."
6 Fold paper toward you three times and place with personal connection items.

Assembly:

1 Cut two pieces of fabric into rectangles or desired pillow shape.
2 Place them together wrong-sides-out and sew three sides.
3 Turn right-side-out and fill halfway with cotton or silk stuffing.
4 Add your herbal mixture, distributing evenly.
5 Place personal connection elements and crystal (if using) in the center.
6 Complete filling with remaining herbs and close the final side.
7 Tie with string in three knots, stating with each knot:
- "Ancestors of my lineage who hold herbal wisdom"
- "I open to your guidance through dream pathways"
- "For healing, wholeness, and recovered knowledge"

Activation Ritual:
1 On the first night of use, place the completed pillow on your altar for several hours before bedtime.
2 Light a white or purple candle and introduce yourself formally to your ancestors, specifically those with herbal knowledge.
3 Share why you seek this connection and how you intend to use the knowledge.
4 Promise appropriate respect and implementation of any wisdom received.
5 Place the pillow under or near your head before sleep.
6 As you drift to sleep, visualize walking backward through your family line, seeing faces of ancestors fading into the distance.

Dreamwork Practice:

1 Keep a dream journal and pen beside your bed for immediate recording upon waking.
2 Record all dreams without initial interpretation, focusing on preservation of content.
3 Note particularly:
- Plants that appear in any form
- Older figures who show or discuss plants
- Locations where healing occurs
- Instructions or recipes provided
- Sensations of taste, smell, or touch related to plants

4 Review entries weekly, looking for patterns or repeated symbols.
5 Research any specific plants or methods mentioned to verify traditional usage.
6 Express gratitude each morning for any guidance received.

Maintenance: Refresh herbal contents every three months or when aroma fades. During refreshing, preserve any personal items while expressing renewed gratitude and intention. Store the pillow wrapped in white cloth when not in use, and keep away from curious children or pets due to potential allergens or small items.

Ethical Considerations: Ancestral dreamwork may reveal practices specific to closed cultural traditions. If you receive information clearly tied to Indigenous or specific cultural healing systems not of your heritage, seek appropriate guidance about ethical engagement with such knowledge rather than immediate implementation or sharing.

Herbal divination encompasses numerous techniques

utilizing plants as both tools for divination and enhancers of divinatory perception. Botanical scrying employs essential oils of clary sage, star anise, or wormwood diffused during mirror or crystal gazing to enhance visual psychic reception. Casting methods utilize plant parts—seeds, nuts, roots, or leaves—as divination pieces, with traditional systems assigning specific meanings to each botanical element. Tea leaf reading specifically works with patterns formed by tea leaves themselves, combining direct plant energy with intuitive symbol interpretation. Smoke reading uses herbal incense or smudge bundles of appropriate plants—mugwort, wormwood, or diviner's sage—creating patterns interpreted for specific guidance. These diverse techniques allow practitioners to select divination methods aligned with both personal affinity and specific inquiry requirements.

Psychic enhancement represents a specialized application of herbs for supporting divination and dream work through temporary augmentation of natural intuitive abilities. Certain herbs traditionally associate with specific psychic centers—eyebright for clairvoyance, calamus for clairaudience, damiana for claircognizance—and can be utilized in appropriate preparations to strengthen these particular abilities. Psychic opening formulas combine herbs like mugwort, star anise, and lemongrass to temporarily increase general receptivity to non-ordinary information. Psychic protection blends incorporating protective herbs like bay, rosemary, and angelica create essential boundaries that prevent energetic vulnerability during states of enhanced openness. These enhancement practices require particular attention to proper dosage, appropriate setting, and clear intention to prevent overwhelming experiences while facilitating effective intuitive reception.

Integration practices transform dream and divination experiences from temporary altered states into lasting wisdom incorporated into waking consciousness and practical magical work. Recording systems create permanent records of received information for later analysis and implementation—dedicated journals specifically designed for documentation, voice recording methods for immediate capture upon waking, or artistic expression translating non-verbal knowledge into tangible form. Analysis techniques help distinguish genuine guidance from subconscious projection—verification through research, cross-referencing across multiple divination methods, or consultation with experienced practitioners. Implementation protocols create appropriate experimental frameworks for testing received information through careful, limited application before broader integration. These integration practices ensure that insights gained through altered states become functional components of ongoing magical development rather than isolated experiences without practical application.

SHAMANIC PLANT PRACTICES

Shamanic plant work represents some of the oldest and most powerful traditions of plant-human relationship, focused on direct spiritual communion and healing through altered states of consciousness. These traditions survive in numerous indigenous cultures worldwide, where specially trained practitioners maintain sophisticated understanding of plants as teachers, healers, and gateways to non-ordinary reality. Contemporary green witches approaching these traditions must balance sincere interest in profound plant relationships with ethical consideration of cultural context, appropriate access, and proper preparation. This section explores responsible approaches to shamanic plant traditions that honor both the power of these practices and the cultures that have preserved them.

Journey space creation using appropriate plants provides containers for spiritual exploration while maintaining necessary protection and boundaries. Safe journey preparations combine gentle aromatic plants that support altered awareness without overwhelming physiological effects—white sage stimulates mental clarity, sweetgrass creates harmony between ordinary and non-ordinary perception, and mugwort gently thins boundaries between worlds. Setting construction establishes both physical and energetic parameters for journey experiences—appropriate location selection, protective circle casting, directional alignments, and intention clarification. Guide relationship establishment creates connections with helping spirits, ancestors, or teachers who provide protection and guidance during journey experiences. These preparatory practices create appropriate containers for exploring altered consciousness while maintaining necessary safety and structure.

Plant teacher relationships within shamanic traditions follow specific protocols developed through generations of ceremonial practice. Initial approach requires appropriate introduction through experienced guides within traditions where such relationships remain active. Preparation often involves extended periods of dietary restriction (dieta), purification practices, and preliminary instruction before direct plant teacher engagement. Ceremonial context provides essential structure through traditional songs, prayers, movements, and community witnessing. Integration support follows direct experiences, with experienced practitioners helping to translate and incorporate received teachings. These traditional frameworks developed specifically to facilitate safe, meaningful relationships with powerful plant teachers while preventing harm through unprepared or inappropriate access.

Ethical engagement with traditional plant knowledge requires careful consideration of multiple factors. Cultural context recognition acknowledges that many shamanic plant practices remain integral aspects of living indigenous traditions rather than abstract spiritual technologies available for individual appropriation. Lineage respect involves understanding that transmission of certain plant relationships traditionally occurs through specific initiated lineages rather than books, workshops, or personal experimentation. Reciprocity practice ensures that engagement with traditional plant knowledge includes tangible support for communities maintaining these traditions through political solidarity, economic support, or direct assistance with plant conservation efforts. These ethical considerations prevent extractive approaches to profound spiritual technologies while creating possibilities for respectful engagement that benefits both practitioners and traditional communities.

Non-appropriative practices allow sincere engagement with shamanic plant principles without cultural theft or disrespect. Bioregional relationships focus on developing shamanic connections with local plants through prolonged direct observation, traditional ecological knowledge appropriate to your region, and gradual, careful experimentation with mild local plants having documented historical usage. Mentorship within appropriate cultural contexts involves finding legitimate teachers who explicitly offer instruction to students outside their tradition, providing fair compensation, and following all guidelines regarding what practices remain closed versus what may be respectfully learned. Contemporary adaptation develops new ceremonial frameworks specifically designed for working with accessible plants in ways that honor traditional principles without mimicking specific indigenous ceremonies. These approaches allow meaningful engagement with profound plant relationships while maintaining ethical boundaries regarding cultural practices.

Sound journey alternatives provide effective access to altered consciousness states without requiring ingestion of powerful plant teachers. Sonic driving using drumming, rattling, and singing at specific frequencies and rhythms creates documented effects on brain wave patterns that facilitate journeying experiences. Movement practices incorporating repetitive motions, specific postures identified in archaeological record, and breath control techniques generate altered consciousness through physiological pathways. Dream incubation working with mild dream-enhancing herbs like mugwort, blue lotus, or Mexican tarragon supports vivid dream journeying within natural sleep cycles. These alternative methods access similar consciousness states while remaining appropriate for practitioners without access to traditional plant teacher relationships or those for whom powerful plant allies are contraindicated.

Through these advanced herbal magic techniques—working with plant spirits and deities, dream and divination practices, and responsible approaches to shamanic traditions—experienced practitioners develop sophisticated relationships with the plant kingdom that transcend basic usage. These practices transform herbs from simple magical ingredients into conscious teachers, allies, and partners in spiritual development. While requiring significant commitment, preparation, and ethical consideration, these advanced techniques offer profound magical experiences that continue the ancient tradition of deep human-plant relationship at the heart of magical herbalism.

GROWING YOUR HERBAL CRAFT

The journey through herbal magic represents not a finite course of study but an ever-evolving relationship with the living plant kingdom. As we conclude this exploration of magical herbalism, we turn toward the ongoing growth of your personal practice—how to deepen your unique plant relationships, document your magical experiences, and continue developing as a steward of botanical wisdom. This lifelong journey transforms initial curiosity into profound partnership with the green world, creating a magical practice as dynamic and ever-changing as the plants themselves.

DEVELOPING YOUR UNIQUE RELATIONSHIP WITH PLANT ALLIES

Throughout this book, we've explored numerous herbal allies and their traditional magical applications. Yet true magical herbalism ultimately transcends standardized correspondences to develop highly personalized relationships with specific plants that resonate with your individual energy, life circumstances, and magical needs. This personalization transforms generic herb usage into authentic magical partnership grounded in direct experience and mutual resonance.

The process of identifying your core plant allies often begins with noticing patterns of attraction and synchronicity. Which plants consistently appear in your environment, dreams, or readings? Which herbs produce particularly potent effects in your magical workings? Which botanical beings evoke immediate emotional or energetic responses upon encounter? These natural attractions often indicate potential for deep magical partnership beyond intellectual selection. By following these intuitive leads while remaining open to unexpected connections, you discover the plants specifically aligned with your magical path.

Deepening these core relationships requires sustained attention and reciprocity. Regular communication through meditation, journaling, and direct care establishes consistent connection. Conscious experimentation with various forms and applications of the same plant—fresh versus dried, root versus leaf, tea versus incense—reveals nuanced understanding of its full spectrum of properties. Seasonal observation of the complete growth cycle, from seed to full expression and back to dormancy, provides insight into the plant's essential nature and timing. These ongoing practices transform initial attraction into profound understanding of specific plant allies.

Personal correspondences often emerge through this dedicated relationship that may differ from traditional associations. While historical correspondences provide valuable starting points, your direct experience remains the ultimate authority on how specific plants function within your unique magical practice. Maintain careful records of these personalized correspondences—noting how particular herbs affect your energy, which magical purposes they best support in your experience, and what preparation methods prove most effective for your work together. This personalized herbal knowledge forms the core of an authentic, effective magical practice aligned with your specific gifts and purposes.

CREATING YOUR PERSONAL HERBAL GRIMOIRE

The creation of a personal magical record represents one of the most valuable practices in herbal witchcraft. This document—whether called a grimoire, Book of Shadows, materia magica, or personal journal—preserves your unique experiences, discoveries, and relationships with plant allies in tangible form. Unlike general herbals or magical texts, this record captures your specific journey with plants, creating both practical reference and magical legacy that grows alongside your practice.

Effective grimoire development combines structured documentation with creative expression. Consider organizing your record through multiple parallel systems—botanical sections documenting individual herbs and their properties; magical categories collecting herbs by purpose (protection, prosperity, healing); seasonal divisions recording observations and workings throughout the yearly cycle; and chronological entries capturing the evolution of your practice over time. This multifaceted organization creates a grimoire that serves various needs while revealing patterns and connections across different aspects of your work.

Documentation of specific magical workings provides both practical reference and opportunity for pattern recognition. Record detailed information about each significant herbal working—plants used and their conditions, astrological timing, preparation methods, ritual components, specific intentions, and subsequent results. Include both immediate outcomes and longer-term manifestations that may emerge days or weeks after the working. This thorough documentation creates accountability while allowing analysis of what approaches prove most effective for particular magical purposes.

Personal discoveries about plant properties often emerge through direct experience that may supplement or occasionally contradict published information. Document these discoveries with particular care—the specific circumstances of your observation, repeated instances that confirm the pattern, and any variations or exceptions noted. These personal insights, developed through direct relationship rather than secondary research, constitute some of the most valuable content in your grimoire, contributing to the living evolution of herbal magical knowledge.

Artistic expression enhances magical records beyond mere information preservation. Consider incorporating botanical illustrations capturing the essential nature of plant allies; pressed specimens preserving physical connections to significant plants; ritual poetry or incantations developed through your practice; and symbolic representations of magical experiences difficult to capture in literal language. These creative elements transform your grimoire from simple reference text into magical tool that engages multiple modes of knowing while deepening your relationship with recorded material.

THE EVOLVING JOURNEY OF THE HERBAL WITCH

The path of herbal magic leads not toward some final state of complete knowledge but rather into ever-deepening relationship with both plants and your own evolving magical nature. Growth in this tradition manifests not primarily through accumulation of information but through transformed perception and relationship—learning to see, feel, and interact with the plant kingdom with increasing subtlety, respect, and reciprocity. This ongoing evolution constitutes the heart of authentic magical herbalism.

Perceptual development represents a crucial aspect of advanced practice. With experience, practitioners typically notice increasing sensitivity to plant energies—ability to discern subtle differences between similar herbs, awareness of how plant properties shift with seasons and growing conditions, and heightened receptivity to direct communication from plant allies. This refined perception transforms magical work from mechanical application of correspondences into nuanced collaboration based on immediate energetic awareness.

Relationship deepening naturally occurs through sustained practice. Initial connections with plant allies typically focus on what properties they offer for specific magical needs. As relationships mature, focus often shifts toward deeper questions—what the plants themselves request of you, how you might serve their purposes and well-being, and where your mutual work intersects with broader ecological and spiritual patterns. This evolution from utilization to partnership characterizes advanced herbal magic, creating relationships of genuine reciprocity and co-creation.

Tradition and innovation maintain necessary balance in evolving practice. Respect for traditional knowledge—carefully preserved through generations of practice and observation—provides essential foundation and context. Simultaneously, changing ecological conditions, cultural contexts, and personal circumstances require thoughtful innovation and adaptation. The mature practitioner navigates this balance with both humility toward traditional wisdom and courage to develop appropriate contemporary expressions of timeless principles.

BECOMING A STEWARD OF PLANT WISDOM AND CONSERVATION

The deepening journey of magical herbalism inevitably leads toward broader ecological awareness and responsibility. As relationships with plant allies strengthen, practitioners naturally develop increased concern for the habitats, conditions, and larger systems that support their botanical partners. This expanding circle of care transforms personal magical practice into environmental stewardship that recognizes the inseparable connection between individual plant relationships and planetary well-being.

Ethical harvesting practices represent the foundation of ecological responsibility. Beyond the basic principles outlined in earlier chapters, advanced practitioners often develop increasingly conservative approaches—harvesting smaller percentages of plant populations, utilizing cultivation rather than wildcrafting for vulnerable species, focusing on invasive plants that benefit from management, and developing deeper relationships with fewer plants rather than constantly seeking new species. These refined approaches minimize impact while maximizing relationship depth.

Habitat preservation and restoration increasingly become natural extensions of plant relationship. Many practitioners evolve from simply using plants to actively creating and protecting the environments they need to thrive—removing invasive competitors, establishing pollinator gardens supporting native plant communities, advocating for protection of wild areas containing important magical species, and supporting land conservation organizations. These activities recognize that truly honoring plant allies requires caring for their broader ecological contexts.

Knowledge preservation balances with appropriate innovation as practitioners develop sufficient experience to contribute to the living tradition of herbal magic. Document unique observations and experiences for future generations, particularly regarding plants native to your bioregion. Share appropriate knowledge with respectful students while maintaining necessary boundaries around information requiring specific preparation or context. Support communities and organizations working to preserve traditional herbal knowledge, especially those led by practitioners from cultures with long histories of specific plant relationships. These preservation efforts ensure that valuable wisdom remains available for future generations while respecting its proper cultural contexts.

Through these ongoing practices—developing personal plant relationships, creating thorough magical records, embracing continuous growth, and engaging in active stewardship—the green witch contributes to an ancient and ever-evolving tradition of human-plant partnership. This living tradition spans countless generations, cultures, and ecosystems, uniting practitioners through the fundamental magical understanding that plants represent not mere objects for human use but conscious allies in creating deeper harmony, healing, and wisdom. May your own journey with herbal magic bring profound connection, effective practice, and joyful discovery for many years to come.

- ***Vivienne Grant***

Printed in Dunstable, United Kingdom